Colin McEvedy **The Penguin Atlas of Modern History (to 1815)**

Maps devised by the author
and lettered by Ivan Atanasoff

Penguin Books

Contents

Introduction

The opening of the modern era is marked by the voyages of discovery. Consequently this atlas, unlike its ancient and medieval companion volumes, cannot make do with a single base map: it requires the use of a world map as well. But it is still Europo-centric – in fact, more so than its predecessors, because the focus is now on Europe not the Europe–Near East area. The rest of the world is considered purely as a stage on which the European struts.

The emphasis on Europe needs no justification. The period was one in which Europeans came to dominate first the high seas, then much of the land area of the globe. They all but eliminated two primitive peoples – the Siberians and Amerindians – and seized their lands. They conquered India and Indonesia. Only the Africans, protected by their poverty and diseases, and the East Asians, still at this stage strong enough to exclude all foreigners, maintained their political integrity. Even so, the Europeans' enormous expansion of the slave trade altered the organization of Africa, and imports of silver and muskets were revolutionary factors in Chinese and Japanese society. The growth of European power is obviously the most significant event of the period.

It is easy to tell the story of Europe's history and its overseas expansion: the main aim of this atlas is to provide a digest of this narrative. But it is also necessary to consider the underlying reasons for the supremacy of the European. I would suggest that this supremacy was based on three interrelated advantages: Europeans were richer than their contemporaries, they were more knowledgeable and they were more flexible. (From where we stand they may seem unbelievably poor, ignorant and rigid, but nevertheless *vis-à-vis* the contemporary extra-European societies, I believe these statements are true.)

The fact that they were richer is probably the primary phenomenon. And as at this time farming was the major human activity and agriculture the main source of wealth, the reason for Europe's prosperity must be sought down on the farm. It is now generally agreed that the 'secret weapon' of the European farmer was the heavy plough. This instrument had been gradually developed during the late Roman and early medieval periods until it was capable of efficiently turning and draining the soils of the high-rainfall zone of North Europe. A series of small improvements in detail and in ancillary equipment, together with an increasing use of other machines – particularly watermills and windmills – kept productivity rising. It was a slow rise, but with the timely help of the Black Death it was enough to keep ahead of population growth. Each medieval century saw Europe a bit wealthier and a bit more efficient at using its wealth.

Economic efficiency correlates with literacy. By the early fifteenth century Europeans were certainly as literate as anyone else, if not more so: in the mid-fifteenth century the invention of movable type printing by Gutenberg of Mainz put Europeans way out in front. Moreover, book production on the new scale made possible by the printing press boosted the demand for information to a level which further improved the supply. From then until the twentieth century the knowledge gap between the West and the rest of the world was to grow at an ever-accelerating rate.

Greater flexibility stems from the first two factors. Basically it is a product of the knowledge that different answers exist, that some are better than others and that better yet remain to be discovered. This attitude is not acquired by illiterate societies, who see what techniques they have as a gift from the gods at the beginning of time.

By the fifteenth century the Europeans had put their wealth, their knowledge and their intellectual flexibility together and created a technology that was more advanced and was developing more rapidly than any other. European successes in the age of discovery and later are often put down purely to these technical advances: if Cortes and Pizarro conquered empires with a handful of men, well, they had guns, hadn't they? In fact the guns were of dubious value. They took so long to reload that most engagements must have become hand-to-hand fights before an arquebusier could fire a second shot. As neither Cortes nor Pizarro had more than a dozen arquebusiers, a dozen will have been about the maximum number of shots fired per battle – hardly a critical contribution in struggles involving thousands. A better case can be made for horses, which were equally unfamiliar and frightening and of far more use; and the best case of all for the steel of the Spanish swords, so much more deadly than the Indians' stone maces and wooden clubs. But one advantage Cortes had, which was of great importance, tends to get neglected in this sort of comparison. The Amerindian fought largely to get captives for sacrifice: personal kudos was won by dashing up to the enemy's line and pulling out a prisoner. The Spaniards fought to destroy the opposing army as a cohesive force. This was a superior concept. So there wasn't just a technological gap between Amerindian and Spaniard – there was also a management gap. Their superior weaponry made the exploits of the *conquistadors* possible: the skill with which this advantage was exploited was the factor that actually created Spain's New World Empire.

The importance of management as well as technical skills in the European success story comes out more clearly in the British conquest of India. At the critical engagement, the battle of Plassey, the disparity in numbers was so great that one immediately assumes that the British victory must have been due to superior equipment. How else could 800 British and 2,200 Indian auxiliaries defeat the army of Bengal, more than 50,000 strong? In fact, as far as fire power is concerned, the advantage lay with the Bengalis: they had fifty-three field-pieces against the British twelve: they also had enough French advisers to get reasonable if less than perfect use out of these guns. Nor was

Plassey a fifth-column victory. Clive improved the battlefield odds by his skilful conduct of the war of intrigue that went on in parallel with the military campaign. The Nabob had come to mistrust his generals and they him. But there was no overt defection until Clive had shown that he could crunch up his enemies on the field of battle. Clive won Plassey and Bengal by the skilful use of extremely meagre resources. He agonized over every decision not only because he had no margin for error in terms of resources but because in the eighteenth century it was in the decision-making process that the ultimate European superiority lay.

Our grasp of a subject becomes secure only when the data can be quantified. Of the three factors we have considered the one which in theory should be easiest to express numerically is wealth. Figures for the gross national product are available for most nations these days and though such figures have their limitations – particularly in the case of isolated economies like Russia's – they give a fair guide to standards of living and national resources. We would be very pleased indeed to have such a series for the early modern period. Unfortunately no reliable figures exist, and attempts to create them are only quantified guesses. We have, however, got revenue figures, and these are of some value. They provide an index of national power which is valid (with reservations) for one particular time and to a lesser extent for comparisons across the whole period. From them we can get a view of the ranking of European nations and of changes in this ranking. I have included these figures in the short essays attached to the economic maps and mentioned some of the reservations to be attached to them. These reservations are sufficiently important to require rehearsing here as well.

1. In the earlier part of our period most European states were still in the process of transition from a feudal order to a money economy. That part of the state's power which could be exerted by custom is not reflected in the revenue figures. It is fair to say that the feudal order was steadily decaying in its usefulness and that states which failed to make the transition – such as Poland – declined into impotence. But in the early part of the period such states could field effective armies and show vigour in their foreign policy.

2. The income figures available are rarely satisfactory to a modern accountant. For some countries they are totally lacking and we have to rely on contemporary estimates of dubious validity. When they exist it is often unclear whether they are in real units or the imaginary units of contemporary accounting practice, whether they represent revenue hoped for or achieved and whether they include the often astronomical costs of collection. Sometimes the coinage was being debased so fast or the government's revenues fluctuating so wildly that a representative figure is a matter of choice rather than calculation.

3. Though occasional debasements are relatively easy to allow for – it is simply a matter of taking an undebased coinage as one's unit – some inflations are not. The inflation that is of major importance is the sixteenth-century price rise caused by the import of silver from the Americas. This not only raised prices in a way that makes comparisons between the beginning and end of the century more than usually treacherous, it raised them at varying rates. Spain inflated fast, England more slowly, so until the silver was evenly distributed a Spanish unit of currency – even when in bullion terms equivalent to an English unit – bought less. Late sixteenth-century figures overrate Spanish resources.

4. In conglomerate states such as the Spanish and Austrian Empires, one has, in theory, to choose between aggregating the total revenues of the constituent states and aggregating the sums remitted by them to the central treasury. If one talks of the revenue of the United States one means the revenue of the federal government, not the revenue of the federal government plus the revenue of the governments of the states. Federal would appear to be the proper meaning for 'Spanish government' revenue. But the Spanish government could use the troops and warships maintained by the Viceroy of Sicily, so it benefited from the local revenues of Sicily. Conversely, much of the central (Castilian) treasury was disbursed in the local government of Castile. The accounts were simply not prepared in a way which yields a 'federal' figure.

I have expressed government revenue during the period 1483–1648 in Venetian gold ducats. The ducat was the standard unit for foreign exchange transactions at the time. It contained 3·5 grammes of pure gold and was never debased. The florin of Florence, the écu (crown) of France and the cruzado of Portugal were of equivalent value: the Burgundian and German florins were of the same weight but only 80 per cent fine and proportionately discounted.[1]

For the period 1648–1815 I have used the £ sterling as my standard unit. By this time the gold/silver ratio had stabilized: the £ was not devalued in terms of either and though sterling refers to silver, Britain was effectively on the gold standard. The switch to the £ is made simply because the £ became the dominant currency of the era and it would be mere pedantry to express the economic transactions of the world in the currency of a petty state. The rate of exchange was 2·1 ducats to the £.

1. All these coins could be used as units of account, i.e. to represent a fixed number of silver coins. Sometimes theoretically equivalent silver coins were minted with the same names. As silver currency was periodically debased and the gold/silver ratio was altering in favour of gold, one has to be careful that when values are expressed in ducats real gold coins are meant. For example, towards the end of the period the Venetian silver ducat had only half the value of the gold ducat.

Before leaving this topic it is necessary to stress that revenue figures give an idea of the power of the state but do not give any indication of *per capita* wealth. The countries of North Europe certainly had relatively high *per capita* incomes at the start of our period, though their *per capita* revenue figures were much lower than Mediterranean countries with more evolved or more ruthless tax-collection systems.

For literacy the obvious quantification is the percentage of the population that can read and write. If we had figures for the period 1500–1815 they would probably show a rise from around 5 per cent to around 50 per cent of adult males in North Europe. An alternative and more reliable quantification is provided by the rise of the book trade. The number of titles published per year, which was around 1,000 at the end of the fifteenth century, had passed the 2,000 mark by the end of the sixteenth. By 1815 it was ten times greater than this: the production rate being around 20,000 titles a year. This series in fact shows up the difference between modern and medieval societies better than the figures for literacy. Take, for example, the comparative figures for a non-progressive state like Turkey. Constantinople got its first printing press in 1726; up to 1815 the total number of titles produced in this, Islam's premier city, was sixty-three. This is equivalent to an annual rate of less than one. The literacy gap between Europe and Turkey (50 per cent and 5 per cent) involves a factor of ten, the publication rate a factor of 10,000. A gap of this size is really an absolute difference, and an absolute difference in terms of social growth is what existed.[1]

When we consider the last of our three factors, intellectual flexibility, we run into a new difficulty. Up to now we have suffered from a lack of data. Now we are in an area where we lack a notation. In the current state of the art there is no scale against which we can measure and grade the intellectual activities of the past. No one can doubt that if the award of Nobel prizes for scientific discovery had begun in the year 1500, from then until the early twentieth century more than 90 per cent of the prizes would have been won by Europeans or individuals from European-derived cultures. But Nobel prizes were not awarded in 1500 and as of now there is really nothing to be said on this topic except that when it does prove possible to assess intellectual activity retrospectively it would be surprising if the figures did not show a gap between Europe and Asia during this period that is so great as to amount to another absolute difference.[2]

The unstated premise in the preceding account of Europe's development in the early modern period is that the development was continuous. Certainly each century had its recessions and slumps and sometimes a particular area – Italy and Spain are examples – could slip backwards over a longer period. But there can be no doubt that taking either Europe as a whole or Northern Europe in particular, prosperity, literacy and knowledge increased every century throughout our period.

This progress seems to me to be the most important single thing about European history, indeed about world history, in the period. So it is curious that whereas some aspects of the process – notably the British 'industrial revolution' of 1780–1815 – have been clearly labelled by historians, the process itself remains nameless. Moreover, it is likely that because of the career structure within which the historians of today operate it will remain nameless for a long time to come, for historians normally restrict themselves to a single century and often to a single generation. On this time scale long-term evolutionary trends are effectively invisible. The swings from boom to slump and back again – on the long view ephemeral and nugatory – appear to historians of the short run with the full magnitude they had for contemporaries. A change in the base line of a few percentage points passes unremarked.

The refusal to look outside the particular society he is studying is one of the historian's great strengths. Nothing is easier or more dangerous than a hindsight emphasis on those elements in a society which only acquire importance later. But an avoidance of teleological thinking and a refusal to consider long-term trends at all are two different things. Inside the short period of time that the historian studies there may be little place for the long perspective: but the long perspective is itself a valid object of study.

Let us take a metaphor from biology. The entomologist studies his insects as animals in their own right, not as halfway houses between viruses and man. But it would be a rare entomologist who did not volunteer that his view of his insects had been greatly enriched by the theory of evolution. He holds in his mind both the special case and the general theory. By contrast the historian is Linnaean: each species of society is to him a special creation, a unique fossil cased in the amber of time.

The attitude is understandable in that no general historical theory of any sophistication exists. Indeed the attempts historians have made to erect comprehensive views of civilization always seem to be anti-evolutionary: societies are seen as individuals that are born, flourish for a day and die, to be replaced by other, near-identical individuals. This

1. The fact that Constantinople's only printing press was closed down from 1730 to 1780 and again in 1800 shows that the difference is not to do with the technology of printing but with society's need for the product. The invention was not only made in Europe (which could possibly be an accident): it succeeded there.

2. The Nobel prizes were first awarded in 1901: the first science prize to go to a non-European was the 1930 physics prize, which was won by the Indian mathematician C. V. Raman. Since then two Chinese and two Japanese have also won physics prizes.

simple anthropomorphism is a very different matter from what has obviously occurred, the continual replacement of one species of society by another which is stronger in some numerical, military or economic sense than its predecessor.

Perhaps the cyclical view reflects the exclusively arts education of historians. Chinese historians, whose education was entirely based on a restricted repertoire of 'classics', created a history of their country which is so dominated by a theory of cycles that it has eliminated almost all trace of the huge differences that existed between successive Chinese empires. A classical education could well predispose to this sort of thinking: everything is measured by a single set of standards: societies rise towards these standards, fall back and then struggle upward again in Sisyphean monotony.

It is probably too early on in the game for anything useful to be done in the way of a general theory. We cannot as yet classify societies properly, let alone do so with the confidence that is essential if the discussion of evolutionary hypotheses is to be meaningful. But the absence of a system for assessing long-term trends is an important fact of present-day historical writing which introduces an element of distortion. For when the trend becomes discernible inside the sort of time interval historians deal with, the significance of this is emphasized out of all proportion. So we get a seventeenth-century 'scientific revolution', and an eighteenth-century 'industrial revolution'. These are real phenomena: but the use of the phrase 'revolution' implies quite incorrect hypotheses about the growth of science and industry. A revolution has a beginning and end: a scientific or industrial revolution must be completed at a certain point in time. Yet no one can believe that the pace of either the scientific or industrial revolutions has slackened since the seventeenth and eighteenth centuries. By every available index the rate of change is still increasing. All that happened in the seventeenth and eighteenth centuries was that the rate of change reached a level at which it

became apparent within a single lifetime, or can be perceived by the historian of a single generation.

A recent newcomer to the series of 'revolutions' which historians perceive within our period is the 'military revolution' of the period 1550–1650. This embraces several phenomena which proceeded hand in hand: a revolution in equipment (the introduction of the arquebus); a revolution in tactics (as an efficient co-operative drill was worked out for arquebusiers and pikemen); a revolution in recruitment (because the new tactics required training to a professional level of skill); and a revolution in scale. Now the revolution in weapons is a revolution of the 'industrial' type – a process that goes back as far as mankind and is still very much with us today. The revolutions in tactics and recruitment are temporary, second-order phenomena. But the change in scale is a different matter. Let us look at it in detail.

In the early sixteenth century the realms of Christendom relied for their defence on the obligation of every fit, adult male to take arms to repel an invader. The number of professional soldiers retained in time of peace was of the order of a few hundred. These few hundred guarded the King's person and garrisoned two or three of the most important royal fortresses. With the appearance of weapons and tactics that demanded a professional level of skill the feudal levy ceased to be an effective part of the state's machinery. However, as the state had not really got the wherewithal to pay for a wholetime standing army the result was that it became near defenceless in peacetime, and fielded only small numbers of men – around 15–30,000 – in wartime. This was so obviously below the potential war-making capacity that every state set out to rectify the situation. Rectified it was in the course of the seventeenth century. The state found new ways to its citizens' pockets and the standing army began to grow at a phenomenal rate. In France, for example, the increase was from the few hundred of the sixteenth century to the 150,000 of the seventeenth. This is a true revolution: within a definite

period of time society shifted gear and having shifted gear the change was complete. Allowing for population growth, France's standing army is roughly the same size today.

It is also a change of no deep significance. As an administrative feat it was within the capacity of such an unprogressive state as the Ottoman. And for that matter it represented only a recovery to the level of administrative competence possessed by the Roman Empire. Whatever factors made European society progressive, the ability to maintain a large standing army was not one of them.[1]

The revolution in land warfare has its parallel at sea. In the course of the seventeenth century the British and other navies grew from a few ships which served as a nucleus around which the merchant galleons gathered in time of war, into permanent fleets which numbered their specialized craft by the dozen. In this instance the long-term trend behind the revolution is clearly visible. Europe's shipping tonnage was steadily mounting, and every century the range, scale and economic importance of the merchant marine increased. The creation of the professional navy was an event: the growth of seaborne trade a continuing process. Can there be any doubt as to which was more important?

All this may seem to be labouring a point too long. My reason is that the phrase 'industrial revolution' has attained such a powerful position in our thinking about the process of industrialization that it merits a full-scale attack. It has, in fact

1. The figures are as follows:

	population (in millions)	standing army (in thousands)	soldiers per 1,000 population
Roman Empire (early 4th century)	c.50	350	7
Ottoman Empire (late 17th century)	c.25	180	7
France (late 17th century)	19	150	8
(1832)	32·5	350	10
(1962)	46·5	415	9

– no mean achievement for a historical theory – done a lot of practical harm. For it is the parent of the economic theory of the 'take-off' – the idea that a stagnant society can be transformed into a progressive one by a short period of intensive capital investment. Following the completion of this forced 'industrial revolution' the economy is supposed to take off into self-sustained growth.

This idea was based on the hypothesis that the era of the 'industrial revolution' was the critical phase in Britain's transformation into a progressive society, and on the observation that during this period Britain was investing a high proportion of its gross national product. The observation is quite true: indeed the generalization that rapid industrialization and a high level of investment go hand in hand is a truism. But Britain's evolution into a progressive society began long before the 'industrial revolution', which merely represented a stage in the maturity of this society. Equating industrialization with progress is as naïve as equating life with breathing: it ignores the period of foetal development in which the mechanism of respiration is created. By the time the baby breathes or the society industrializes the real work of development is done.

The evolution of the progressive society in Europe – for Britain was only the first in a flotilla of countries sailing this course – is the very stuff of history. But it is surely not the right process for today's underdeveloped countries to study. Its details are arguable where they are not totally obscure, and the whole development took centuries. The underdeveloped country needs a clearer model and a quicker result. This exists in Japan, which in a very short period – roughly the years between 1868 and 1889 – transformed itself from a stagnant to a progressive society. No one can deny the revolutionary status of these two decades, for Japan has been a successful industrial society ever since. And anyone can see that the revolution was *social*, involving the exchange of old ideas and aims for new ones of European inspira-

tion. Only after this did the country begin to industrialize.

The take-off hypothesis dominated development theory in the years after the Second World War. It encouraged poor nations to beg, borrow or steal as much money as they could. Its results have been lamentable. Many underdeveloped nations are now weighted down with such a heavy external debt that their chances of getting airborne have diminished, not increased. The experiment has merely made it clear that it is new attitudes that the underdeveloped nations must import. Abandoning cherished beliefs is a more painful process than borrowing money. However, the underdeveloped can at least be thankful that, unlike a failing animal species, they can give themselves a second chance by adopting the features of their more successful rivals.

In the preparation of the first two volumes in this series I had the advantage of frequent discussions with Peter Fison. Shortly after I began work on the present volume he contracted leukemia and in 1969, at the age of forty, he died. Many people have helped me since then, but no one could take his place: this book is dedicated to the memory of this shrewd, noisy, vital man.

The Atlas

The World in 1483
1. Population

No species is uniformly distributed across its habitat, but mankind is unique in having a 10,000-year history of increasingly uneven distribution. In the last century and a half the driving force behind this process has clearly been industrialization, and the expression has taken the form of urban concentration. In the centuries prior to the nineteenth, however, industry and towns had only marginal demographic significance. Variations in population density were a function of agricultural productivity.

Climate and know-how are the factors that govern agricultural productivity: irrigating techniques in a hot country provide the maximum return. So in the fifteenth century the range of population densities had at its top end countries like Egypt, where densities per square mile had long been in the hundreds. Temperate agriculture supported densities in the tens, and herding – the pastoral way of life characteristic of the Asian steppe – densities in single figures. Pure food-gatherers probably averaged only 1 to every 10 square miles of their range.

In the Old World there were three main agricultural areas: Europe, with about 70–75 million people, India with 100–120 million (very high density in the Ganges valley) and China with 110–130 million (very high densities in the Hwang Ho and Yangtze Kiang valleys). Between Europe and India lay the Near Eastern countries with high-density islands of peasants set in an arid landscape occupied by nomadic herdsmen. This zone contained about 20–30 million people of whom 2–3 million were nomads. The major agricultural areas can thus be visualized as (1) a band covering continental Europe (and the southern shore of the Mediterranean), the Near East (weaker in numbers and lacking continuity) and India: (2) a separate East Asian area centred on China but including Japan (with about 15 million inhabitants), Korea

(3 million) and Vietnam (3 million). There were farmers in the rest of South-East Asia and in the Philippines and Indonesia, but even given the technology of the era this zone was markedly underpopulated. The only other agricultural area of significance was Africa south of the Sahara. Population figures here are exceedingly speculative, but something of the order of 25–35 million is a reasonable guess, the Western Sudan having a density twice that of the remainder.

The nomad in pure culture dominated the Asian pasture lands. These stretched from the South Russian steppe via Turkestan to Mongolia and Manchuria. Counting in Tibet to the south, something like 5 million nomads were able to support themselves on this extensive range and keep farmers off the parts of it that were suitable for agriculture.

The pre-Columban inhabitants of the New World had not domesticated any animals of significance,[1] so the pastoral style was lacking in the Americas. In Mexico a sophisticated irrigating agriculture supported a sizable population: the rest of Central America was also fairly well populated, as was the Andean spine of South America. Elsewhere there were scattered tribes of primitive agriculturalists or semi-agriculturalists, shading off into food-gatherers in the west of America and in Canada to the north, and in Chile and the Argentine to the south. Central America contained perhaps 5 million people, the continent as a whole perhaps 11 million.[2]

As for the food-gatherers, one million each for the New World, Asia and Indonesia–Australia would be generous. This is less than 1 per cent of the world total suggested by all these figures, which add up to something over 400 million.

1. The Peruvians had tamed the llama: they used it as a (most inefficient) pack animal and sheared the fleece of the related alpaca.

2. Much higher figures have been bandied about recently and though I do not think Mexico's population can ever have reached the 15–20 millions proposed by some, there is a strong suggestion that population in Central America was subject to big swings. One such boom-and-bust cycle had left the southern (Mayan) zone permanently bust by the tenth century: another bust may have been pending in the Central Mexican area when the Spaniards arrived. On this view the Aztecs' bloody religious rites (which consumed up to 20,000 people a year) could represent an adaptive response to an over-population problem.

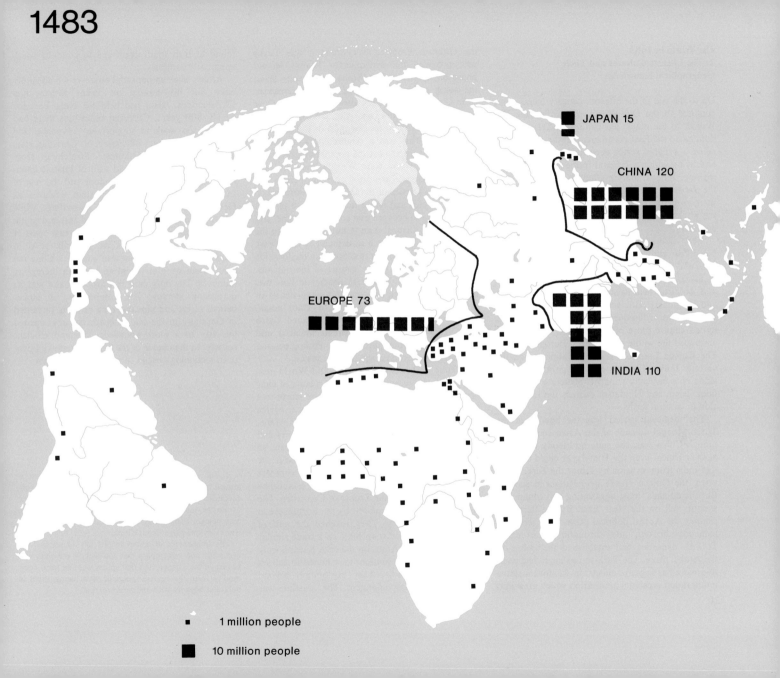

1483

JAPAN 15

CHINA 120

EUROPE 73

INDIA 110

■ 1 million people

■ 10 million people

2. The Literate Cultures and Their Geographical Knowledge

Up to the end of the fifteenth century literacy was confined to the Old World and, within the Old World, to the major agricultural societies. China dominated the East Asian area, all the East Asians using a syllabic script derived from the Chinese and living within a cultural framework of Chinese making. Indeed, among China's neighbours only the Japanese felt they had a national identity of their own – the rest accepted China as the centre of the world and the sole legitimate source of political authority.

Very different was the situation in Europe, the Near East and India. The elongated shape of this zone and the fact that the weight of population was at the ends, not in the middle, made for cultural and political heterogeneity. Alphabetical scripts and religious fanaticism are about its only common factors. Consequently, whereas China was a united empire more often than not, no state ever embraced the whole stretch from Europe to India. The Roman Empire, the Arab Caliphate and the various Indian Empires are the political expressions of a basically tripartite structure. Christendom, Islam and Hinduism express the same division in cultural terms.

The medieval period was the heyday of the Turco-Mongol nomads of the Asian steppe. Huge though China was, she suffered bloody conquests at their hands: even the Himalayas could not protect India from invasion by Timur the Turk. Westward, the Golden Horde held Russia in slavery. But the nomads' most devastating and continuous assaults fell on the Near East. By the thirteenth century the Arabs' political power had been permanently broken, and throughout the region Turkish dynasties had established themselves in the Arabs' place. The Turkish onslaught had positive as well as negative effects: in Anatolia massive immigration created a new nation which grew into the Ottoman Empire: everywhere it was Turks who provided the dynamic for Islam's second phase of expansion. The Arabs had already taken the south and east shores of the Mediterranean from Christendom and the lower Indus valley from the Hindus. The Turks took South Russia and the Balkans and brought the conquest of India near to completion. This was a remarkable achievement which went right against the population gradients.

Neither Old nor New Worlds knew of each other's existence in the pre-Columban period, but the literate societies of the Old World were linked by trade routes and had a fair knowledge of each other. One path between east and west was the 'silk route' across Central Asia (Chinese silk, being the world's finest, was much in demand in the West). Its vitality – in the fifteenth century on the low side – varied according to the temper of the nomads. More important in scale and steadier in flow was the sea traffic along the east and south coasts of Asia, where an overlapping series of Arab, Indian, Chinese and Japanese shippers connected Cairo and Nagasaki via Aden, Calicut, Malacca and Canton. Branch routes brought the Philippines and the Indonesian archipelago into the system.[1]

Thanks to this trade network, Old World geographers had a reasonably accurate picture of their hemisphere. The missing pieces were north-east Siberia, and Central and Southern Africa. Africa was the more intriguing. For centuries trans-Saharan caravans had brought gold dust, ivory and slaves from the Sudan to the Mediterranean, so there was some information available about the Niger basin. And on the east coast Arab traders seeking the same commodities had established posts as far south as the Tropic of Capricorn. The west coast was first explored by the Portuguese in the fifteenth century. They reached the gulf of Guinea in 1471 and soon built up a trade similar to that run by the Arabs on the east. But this only satisfied half their ambition: they hoped to sail on past Africa to India. Alas, exploration beyond Guinea was a disappointment. The coastline was found to turn south again and to continue south apparently endlessly.

At this stage an impartial observer would surely have put his money on Islam rather than Christendom. Islam had held the Near East for nearly 800 years, Christian minorities there had become too weak to support any revanche, and anyhow, for military efficiency, no Christian state could match the Ottoman. Stretching from Morocco to Kazan, a solid wall of Islamic countries stood between Christendom and the rest of the known world. Such Christian enclaves as Georgia and Abyssinia were dwindling, while Islam's steady expansion continued east and south. The Negroes of the Niger and of the east coast of Africa, the oasis-dwellers on the silk road in Turkestan and the Indonesean islanders along the spice route were all adopting Islam in increasing numbers. The only card in Europe's hand was its increasing literacy. The combination of alphabetical script and movable-type printing (invented in Germany in the mid fifteenth century) opened the way to a more knowledgeable and efficient society. In the course of the fifteenth century European technology began to pull ahead of Asian.

1. The sea lane from the East to the Near East is known as the spice route. Many of the spices came from Indonesia – cloves and nutmeg specifically from the Moluccas, mace and camphor from other islands in the archipelago. Pepper came mostly from India, cinnamon from Ceylon, ginger from China.

The importance of spices in this period seems ludicrous till one remembers that the diet of the time was boring in the extreme and that spices were an ideal commodity from the traders' point of view, being small in bulk, but high in price and profit margin.

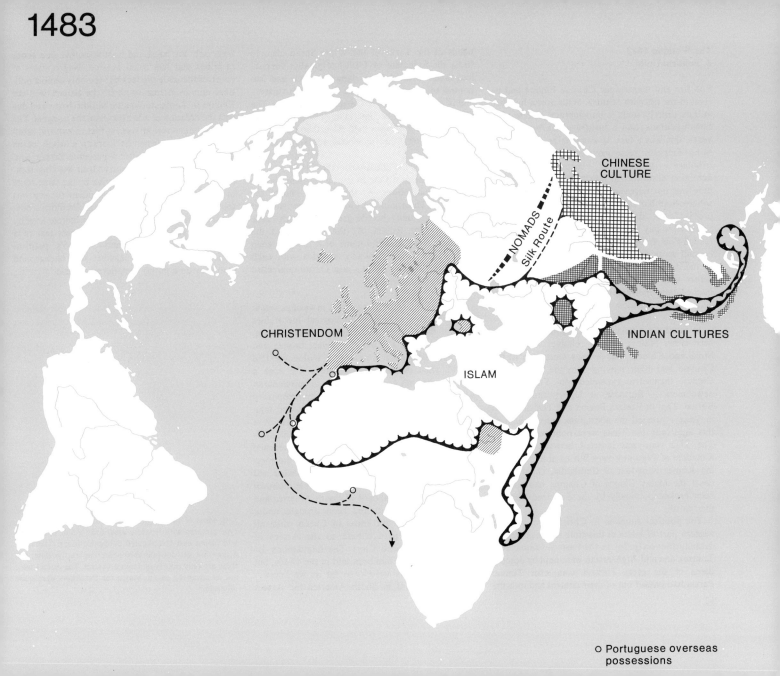

1483

CHINESE
CULTURE

NOMADS

Silk Route

CHRISTENDOM

INDIAN CULTURES

ISLAM

O Portuguese overseas
possessions

For size and majesty the Chinese Empire had no rival in the fifteenth century. With over a hundred million orderly souls, a bureaucracy of indestructible traditions, and a history going back 3,000 years, this was a fact. It was also an attitude: the Ming Emperor recognized other states only as tributary – or rebellious – members of a world dominion bestowed on him by Heaven. This attitude was not unreasonable within the East Asian sphere: both Korea and Vietnam had been Chinese provinces in the past and their rulers were prepared to pay token tribute in return for Chinese recognition. It became untenable when the world beyond became visible and was then to cause a loss of the dignity it was supposed to enhance. Even before that happened it had done damage as an intellectual soporific, making the Chinese smug and incurious, and lowering the vitality of their culture.

In South-East Asia the original inhabitants had been either Malays or near relatives such as the Mons and Khmers, but peoples more akin to the Chinese had been moving into the area as the Chinese themselves expanded into Yunnan. The newcomers – Burmese in Upper and Central Burma, Thai in Eastern Burma and Thailand, Lao in Laos – pressed the aborigines hard, though at this date only the Thais were politically unified. The Thai state was inserted between the Mon Kingdom of Pegu in Lower Burma and the declining Khmer Kingdom of Cambodia. On the east coast the Malay Chams of Champa had already been broken politically by the Sinicized Viets to their north.

The political situation in Christendom and the western part of Islam at this time is considered in detail further on (p. 26). In the Eastern Islamic area Transoxiana and Afghanistan were held by descendants of the great Turkish conqueror Timur; Persia had passed out of their control and into the hands of the Turks of the White Sheep clan. In India the Sultanate of Delhi, originally Turkish, had fallen to an Afghan dynasty which had lost control of everything outside the Ganges valley – and of Bengal (the lower Ganges area) as well. The old provinces had become independent kingdoms, while resurgent Hindus held Rajasthan and, in the extreme south, the unconquered Kingdom of Vijayanagar.

In one way the situation in the 1480s was unusual: for the first time in centuries there was no major nomad power. At the western end of the steppe the Tartars of the Golden Horde had split into four mutually hostile groups – which made life easier for Russia. At the eastern end the Chinese played a skilful game of bribery to keep the Mongol tribes similarly at odds with each other. In between, Kazaks and Oirats quarrelled without benefit of subsidy.

Cultural level can be assessed in various ways: the archaeologist likes technological hierarchies because the material obtained by excavation immediately places the culture: stone, bronze and iron ages provide a simple and, within the Old World, valid evolutionary sequence. On such a view the fifteenth-century Negroes of sub-Saharan Africa comfortably outrank the contemporary Amerindians, for whereas the Negroes had long been an Iron Age people, the Amerindians were without useful metals of any kind. The ranking is misleading: socially the Amerindians had reached a level at least equivalent to the Negro. In the areas where there were enough of them – Mexico and Peru – they had erected considerable political units: the Pacific seaboard of South America and its Andean hinterland had been brought under unified control by the Incas of Cuzco while all Central Mexico paid tribute to the Aztecs of Tenochtitlan (Mexico City). The foundations for both these empires had been laid in the 1440s, but whereas the Incas were – so far as we know – without precedent in South America the Aztecs were only the latest and least attractive in a series of tribes that had ruled Mexico. Negro states of comparable scale are lacking: the only sizable political unit in Africa south of the Sahara was the Empire of Timbuctoo on the Middle Niger and this was the creation of a Berber clan, the Songhai. The Middle Niger region was, in fact, a cultural satellite of North Africa, its literacy a result of its conversion to Islam after a previous Berber conquest in the eleventh century. Iron-working techniques had reached Black Africa by the same route in the first century B.C. Amerindian society was too far away to receive any such Pandora's box, but the Mexicans did get to a proto-literate level by their own efforts. Literacy is the best test of a society's sophistication and Mexico's political achievements fit better against this background than they do a purely metallurgical scale.[1]

---

1. Most of the Mayan 'inscriptions' are comic-strip-type pictures with heraldic identifications of individuals and places and complicated dating formulae. There are a few that get considerably nearer to true writing, but these are only poorly understood as yet. The Aztecs were not as advanced as the Maya; the Peruvians were quite illiterate.

1483

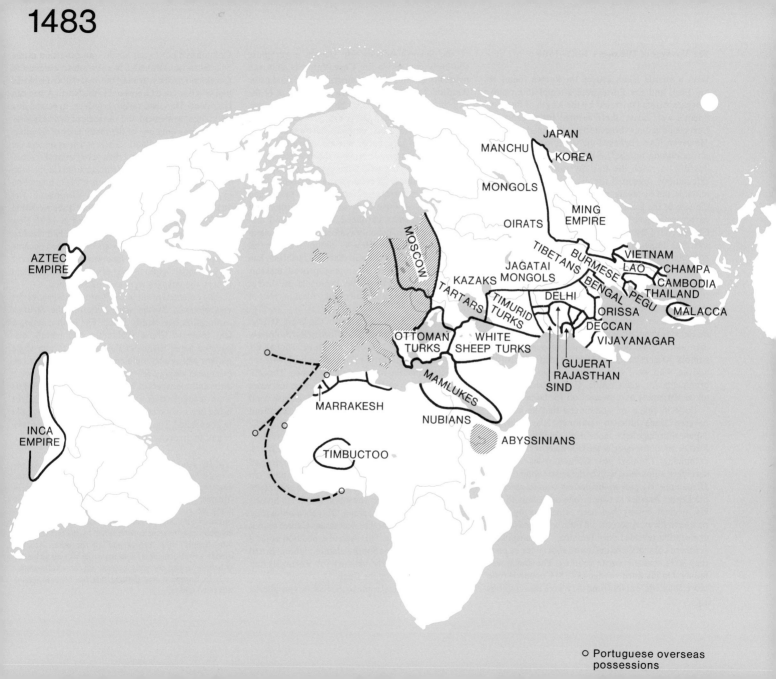

AZTEC EMPIRE

INCA EMPIRE

MOSCOW

TARTARS

OTTOMAN TURKS

MARRAKESH

MAMLUKES

NUBIANS

TIMBUCTOO

ABYSSINIANS

KAZAKS

TIMURID TURKS

WHITE SHEEP TURKS

JAGATAI MONGOLS

DELHI

SIND

RAJASTHAN

GUJERAT

DECCAN

VIJAYANAGAR

ORISSA

BENGAL

TIBETANS

BURMESE

PEGU

LAO

VIETNAM

CHAMPA

CAMBODIA

THAILAND

MALACCA

OIRATS

MONGOLS

MING EMPIRE

MANCHU

KOREA

JAPAN

o Portuguese overseas possessions

The Voyages of Discovery 1487–1500

With a hostile Islam astride the known routes to the East, and the Portuguese attempt to circumnavigate Africa frustrated by the length of the continent's west coast, there seemed little chance of Europeans gaining direct access to oriental markets. However, if you believed the world was round – as an increasing number of people did – it might be possible to reach the East by sailing west. Most calculations suggested the distances would be formidable, but by taking the largest current estimate of the size of the Eurasian land mass and the smallest current estimate of the size of the globe the Genovese, Christopher Columbus, managed to convince himself that Japan lay only 3,000 miles across the Atlantic. He obtained the backing of Ferdinand and Isabella of Spain and in 1492 put his arithmetic to the test. If he was a second-rate geographer he was a first-rate sailor. Setting out from the Canaries with three ships he arrived at the islet of San Salvador in the Bahamas after thirty-three days on the open sea. He threaded his way through the Bahamas to Cuba, and then sailed east along its northern coast to Hispaniola. After establishing friendly relations with the natives, who were very willing to trade their gold ornaments for glass beads, Columbus founded a token settlement and then set off for home.[1]

Back in Spain he announced that he had discovered some hitherto unknown islands in the Japanese archipelago: Japan itself could not be much further on. In the interim the new discoveries needed colonizing. The next year Columbus led a fleet of seventeen ships filled with enthusiastic volunteers to Hispaniola. He picked the perfect course, reaching the Lesser Antilles in twenty-one days, only to find his original colony had been wiped out by exasperated natives. A second did little better and further exploration revealed only Jamaica, the inhospitable southern coast of Cuba and more aborigines, so poor they were scarcely worth robbing. The dream was fading. On his third voyage (1498) Columbus took more colonists, but this time they were the scrapings

of the Spanish prisons. He steered a yet more southerly course via the Cape Verde Islands and made his landfall at the southernmost of the Lesser Antilles, Trinidad. After a brief exploration of the adjacent mainland – which he recognized as continental by the size of the rivers – he made for the colony on Hispaniola, now moved by his brother Bartholomew to a better site on the south coast (present San Domingo). None of the three Columbus brothers were successful administrators; there was constant trouble in the colony and a royal official sent out in 1500 to investigate complaints was so shocked that he sent all three back to Spain in irons. The Spanish monarchs pardoned Columbus and employed him again, but only as an explorer. His fourth and last voyage (1502–4) along the Central American coastline showed that the Caribbean Sea was closed on the west. His report 'proved' that this stretch of land was the Malay Peninsula. He died in 1506, full of grievances and cranky ideas, a relic of the pre-Columban age.

The Portuguese exploration of the West African coastline finally paid off in 1487 when Bartholomew Diaz rounded the Cape of Good Hope. Though his men refused to go further Diaz sailed back with the conviction that the route to India lay open. The full-scale expedition of Vasco da Gama came ten years later. To take advantage of the anti-clockwise wind system of the South Atlantic, da Gama stood well out from Africa, turning east only when he reckoned he had reached the latitude of the Cape. He slightly miscalculated, making an accidental landfall a hundred miles north of the Cape, but thereafter had plain sailing and arrived in Southern India ten months after leaving Lisbon. Despite the hostility of the local Moslem traders he was able to carry home a cargo of pepper and cinnamon. Only six months after da Gama's return another fleet under Cabral set out to repeat his voyage. This second expedition sailed a wider arc through the South Atlantic, sighting Brazil (which was promptly claimed for Portugal) and comfortably clearing the Cape.

A third theoretical route to the East was parallel to

Columbus's but to the north – an extension of the ancient and still-travelled Norse route to Iceland and Greenland. Briefly, around the year 1000 the Norse had sailed beyond Greenland to the North American continent. They had failed, however, to establish a permanent settlement and the saga of their exploration became only one of the many tales of fabulous islands in the far Atlantic. Tales spurious or genuine probably played less part than geographical reasoning in the thinking of the Venetian John Cabot, who persuaded the English King Henry VII to finance an exploration of the seas beyond Greenland. His voyages are poorly documented, but it seems that in 1497 he reached Newfoundland and in 1498 New England. He dutifully reported that he had reached the territory of the Great Khan,[2] but it soon became apparent that this barren land was no China. Except for seasonal exploitation of the Newfoundland fishery the voyages were not followed up.

The potential profit in the Portuguese discoveries was obvious. By the same criterion the Spanish exploration had clearly failed. Far from opening a fast route to China, Columbus had merely discovered some islands of dubious worth and some natives whose accumulated stock of gold was to be exhausted within a few years. But these islands were only a minor aspect of what everyone but Columbus soon recognized as a New World: any day might bring news of a country where there really was gold in abundance. The gullible, the greedy and the brave began the search for El Dorado.

1. He returned on a more northerly route via the Azores. On both outward and return voyages he made near perfect use of the clockwise winds of the North Atlantic, which suggest that either he knew what he was doing or else was extraordinarily lucky. Though his choice of the Canaries rather than the Azores as a starting point may have been determined by the fact that they were Spanish (the Azores and all the other Atlantic islands were Portuguese) it seems easier as well as kinder to believe he had correctly worked out the wind system.

2. In Europe it was thought that the Mongol Khans still ruled China.

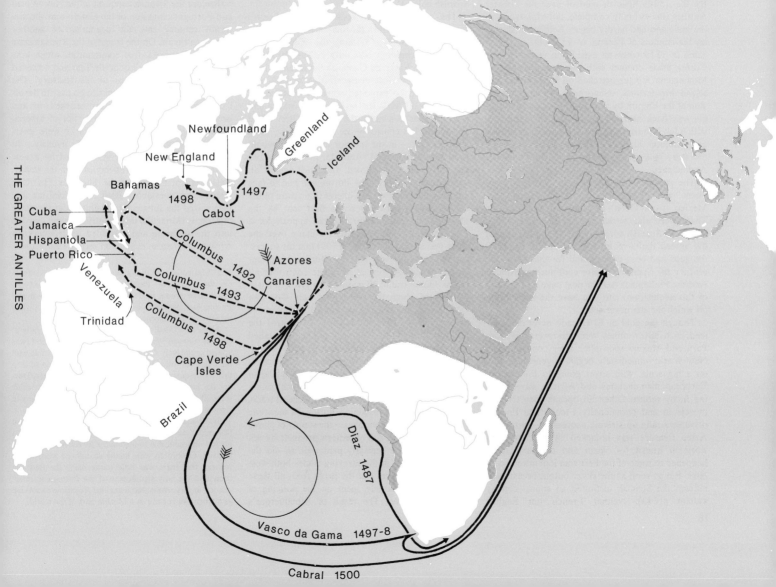

THE VOYAGES
OF DISCOVERY 1487-1500

THE GREATER ANTILLES

Newfoundland

Greenland

Iceland

New England

Bahamas

1498

1497

Cuba

Jamaica

Cabot

Hispaniola

Columbus 1492

Puerto Rico

Azores

Venezuela

Columbus 1493

Canaries

Trinidad

Columbus 1498

Cape Verde
Isles

Brazil

Diaz 1487

Vasco da Gama 1497-8

Cabral 1500

The World in 1600
1. Political Units

By the 1520s Spanish control over the Greater Antilles was virtually complete, but exploration of the mainland had hardly begun. Settlement started on the isthmus of Panama in 1510: the real push came in 1519 when an expedition under Hernan Cortez made contact with the Aztec Empire of Montezuma. Cortez marched on Mexico City and seized Montezuma, temporarily winning possession of the Empire by this coup. Ejected, he fought his way back into the capital the next year and, with a few hundred men, made himself master of as many million. Sixteen years later Pizarro repeated the story in Peru by capturing the Inca emperor Atahualpa.

The pattern of entry into the American continent was thus: Panama (from Hispaniola), Mexico (from Cuba) and Peru (from Panama). There were also settlements on the River Plate, which the Spanish correctly calculated lay beyond the agreed limits of Portuguese Brazil. By 1550 the gaps had been filled in and for the rest of the century the Spanish Empire continued to expand. Add the Philippines (see the next page for the story of this acquisition) and you have the first empire on which the sun never set.[1]

Though the gold of El Dorado never materialized, rich silver mines were discovered in both Peru and Mexico soon after their conquest. The New World immediately began to generate traffic on a big scale, with silver going to Europe and European manufactures and African slaves coming in by return. Other Europeans soon tried to muscle in and occasionally French and English privateers rang up striking successes – part of the Aztec treasure was hi-jacked by a Frenchman while in transit for Spain and the same thing happened to some of the Peruvian loot fifteen years later. But as soon as the silver output became significant the Spanish instituted an annual convoy system (1543). Neither French nor English

attempted to stand in the way of these convoys: their activities were limited to picking off unescorted merchantmen and attacking isolated Spanish colonial settlements.[2]

The vast territorial acquisitions of Spain's *conquistador* era reflect the total inferiority of New World technology. Within the Old World, European technology was only marginally superior to Asian. Vasco da Gama on his second trip to India gave a perfect demonstration of how this margin could be exploited when he destroyed a native fleet off Malabar: he kept his distance and used his guns at a range the native artillery could not match. But control of the coasts was the most he hoped for – in the interior he knew he would soon be overwhelmed. Almeida, first Portuguese viceroy in the East, agreed, and ruled against all commitments ashore. The Portuguese had to face not only the seapower of Gujerat (the centre of the native trading network) but a fleet sent by the Mamlukes in response to Gujerati appeals for a Moslem Holy War. Almeida's victory over the allies was so complete (Diu, 1509) that his successor Albuquerque was able to afford a more ambitious policy. Aiming at complete control of all Indian Ocean traffic he organized a girdling chain of forts of which the lynch pins were Goa (the viceregal capital), Ormuz (to control the mouth of the Persian Gulf) and Malacca (to control the Malayan Straits). Between these points ships sailed with Portuguese permission or at their peril.[3] Simultaneously the exploration was pushed further east to the Spice Islands (1512), China (1513) and Japan (1543). Here there was no chance of controlling the routes but considerable profit in general trade.

Of the elements sustaining Portugal's maritime empire two were monopolies – the supply of slaves to the New World and of eastern products by sea to Europe. These certainly paid well, as did the Portuguese share in the carrying trades both west and east of Malacca. But the profit from all these operations was largely spent on the policing of the Indian Ocean. The result of Albuquerque's

brilliantly conceived and executed strategy seems to have been more empire than Portugal could comfortably afford.

Besides the Spanish conquest of the New World and Portugal's invasion of the eastern seas the sixteenth century saw the beginning of another European thrust. On the fringe of the Russian state were the Cossacks, free communities which acknowledged the suzerainty of the Tsar and defended his frontier without cost to his treasury. The arquebus enabled the Cossacks to go over to the offensive and in the 1590s they crossed the Urals and presented the Tsar with his first slice of Siberia.

In Persia the White Sheep Turks were overthrown by the native Safavid dynasty. In Transoxiana Timurid rule was erased by a new wave of (Uzbek) Turks moving in from the steppe. This was not the end of the Timurids. One clan managed to re-establish itself in Afghanistan and then seized the sultanate of Delhi: under the name of Moguls (Mongols) this Timurid line put new life into the sultanate and expanded its frontiers. In Africa a Moroccan expedition seized Timbuctoo.

1. You could add in a great deal more than is shown on the map, for Philip II of Spain obtained the Portuguese crown in 1580. However the Spanish and Portuguese overseas Empires remained legally and actually distinct throughout the period of union.
2. Up to 1559 France and Spain were continually at war in Europe: privateering during this period was almost exclusively French. English attempts to trade with the colonists followed and Spain's determination to stop this traffic quickly transformed traders into pirates. During the last quarter of the century the important raids were all mounted for England, with the Dutch joining in right at the end.
3. Albuquerque originally intended to control the Red Sea outlet as well, but he failed to take Aden and it proved impracticable to maintain a garrison on waterless Socotra. Operations were finally abandoned when it was realized that there was little traffic using the Red Sea route and the only significance of the Portuguese intervention in this area is that it enabled Abyssinia to survive as a Christian enclave in a Muslim part of the world.

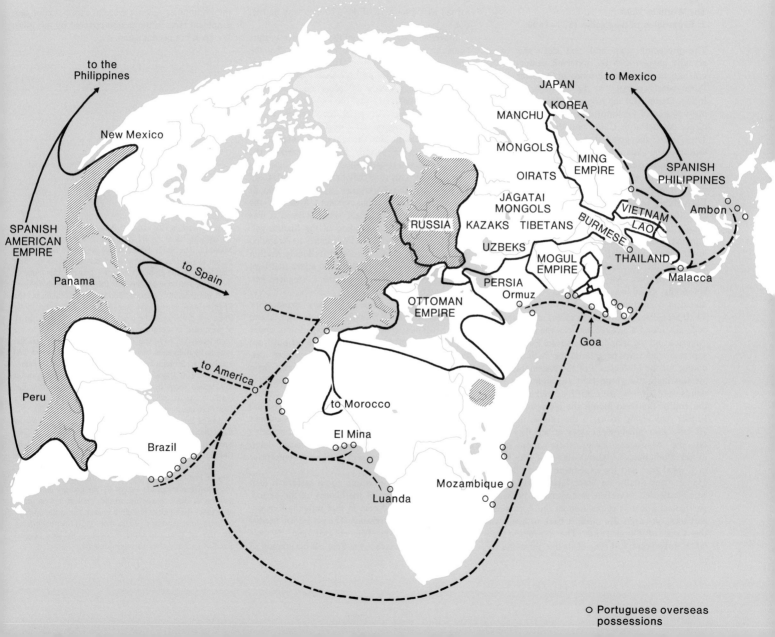

1600

to the
Philippines

New Mexico

SPANISH
AMERICAN
EMPIRE

Panama

to Spain

Peru

Brazil

to America

to Morocco

El Mina

Luanda

Mozambique

RUSSIA

OTTOMAN
EMPIRE

PERSIA
Ormuz

UZBEKS

KAZAKS

JAGATAI
MONGOLS

OIRATS

MONGOLS

MANCHU

JAPAN

KOREA

MING
EMPIRE

TIBETANS

BURMESE

MOGUL
EMPIRE

Goa

VIETNAM
LAO

THAILAND

Malacca

to Mexico

SPANISH
PHILIPPINES

Ambon

○ Portuguese overseas
possessions

The World in 1600
2. Exploration of the Pacific 1521–1600

The preceding map and text deal with what actually happened in the sixteenth century – the creation of a Spanish Empire in America and a Portuguese hegemony in the South Atlantic and Indian Ocean. But the original impulse behind all the voyages of exploration had been the hope of direct contact with China and the Spice Islands. These were the goals that really sparkled with wealth. The Spanish pre-occupation with the Orient survived the discovery of the Americas and, in a small way, distorted the simple division of the world into Portuguese and Spanish spheres. The Portuguese, as we have seen, reached the Spice Islands and China in 1513. In the same year the *conquistador* Balboa crossed the Isthmus of Panama to discover the Pacific and put Spain back in the race to the Far East.

The Pacific was the factor that made sense of the new discoveries. All that Columbus had said before he sailed was going to be true, but the distances needed multiplying by two. Or more? In 1520 Magellan, a Portuguese sailing in the service of Spain, found a passage between the tip of South America and the island of Tierra del Fuego. With supreme confidence he entered the Pacific and set course for the Moluccas. For the first month morale was high, though no land was sighted and the winds were carrying them north as well as west. By the end of the third month the crew were eating leather and trying to catch the rats in the hold. At last, after ninety-eight days at sea they came on the Marianas. From there they sailed to the Philippines – where Magellan was killed in a local war and the expedition nearly disintegrated – and finally the Spice Islands. Del Cano, who succeeded Magellan in command, built and garrisoned a fort in opposition to the Portuguese and took on cargo. He made it back to Spain via the Cape of Good Hope. The expedition had taken three years, lost four of its five ships and returned with a bare 18 of the 270 men who had set out.[1]

Magellan's voyage proved that the Spice Islands could be reached across the Pacific, not that the new route was competitive. The various disasters that overtook two follow-up expeditions (one from Spain via the Straits of Magellan, one from Mexico) demonstrated that the logistics were all in Portugal's favour. In 1529 the Spanish wisely accepted a Portuguese offer of 350,000 ducats to forget the claim. But though the Spanish abandoned the Spice Islands they remembered the Philippines, and a generation later they occupied them (1565). This time they held an ace – Mexican silver – and the Portuguese were pleased to fit them into their trading system. Although the resulting trans-Pacific trade was not large it was steady and the annual sailing of the Manila galleons (from Manila in the Philippines to Acapulco in Mexico and back) continued its lonely rhythm for two centuries. It was Mexican silver that kept Macao alive after the rest of the Portuguese network had been destroyed.[2]

The Spaniards made one more exploratory effort in the Pacific. Stimulated by an Inca legend of rich islands in the west, an expedition under the command of Alvaro de Mendana set out from Peru in 1567. Mendana sailed due west, discovered the Solomon Islands and thought them worth colonizing. It took him till 1595 to get a second expedition fitted out and this time he could not find the Solomons. (The next person who did was the Englishman Carteret in 1767.) His attempt to settle Santa Cruz failed – as did his lieutenant's attempt to settle Espiritu Santo a decade later. On this dead note the saga of Spanish enterprise ended.

In choosing a projection for a historical map one is taking a view of the history of the period. The standard world map in this series is Europocentric for obvious reasons. The projection needed to record the Magellan episode and its sole political consequence – the Spanish occupation of the Philippines – is not a useful expression of geographical facts in the period covered by this atlas. We shall not need it again.

1. Earlier in his career Magellan had sailed the Portuguese route to the East and got at least as far as Malacca. The Spice Island native whom he bought as a personal slave at that time presumably became the first man to circle the globe, though it is possible that some of the European crew had been in the Spice Islands before.

2. Immediately after Columbus's first voyage the Spanish and Portuguese had negotiated – through the Pope – a division of the world based on Spain's priority in westward exploration and Portugal's eastward. In the final treaty of 1494 the Portuguese managed to get the longitudinal division between the two spheres placed 370 leagues (1,100 nautical miles) west of the Azores rather than the 100 leagues originally proposed. In the event this netted them Brazil, a bit of good fortune that has made some suspect the Portuguese had sighted the Brazilian coast before its official discovery in 1500.

As for the Spice Islands, Portugal claimed that as she had reached them *first* by sailing *east* they were hers. The Spanish said the dividing line ran right round the globe (longitude 45°W being complemented by 135°E) and that the Spice Islands lay just on their side of it. In fact they lie just on the Portuguese side, but there was no way of measuring longitude except by the grossly inaccurate process of dead reckoning, so the Spanish had an arguable case. Better than arguable in fact, for in the opinion of most contemporary geographers (still over-estimating the size of Asia and under-estimating the new-fangled Pacific) 135°E passed through Malaya.

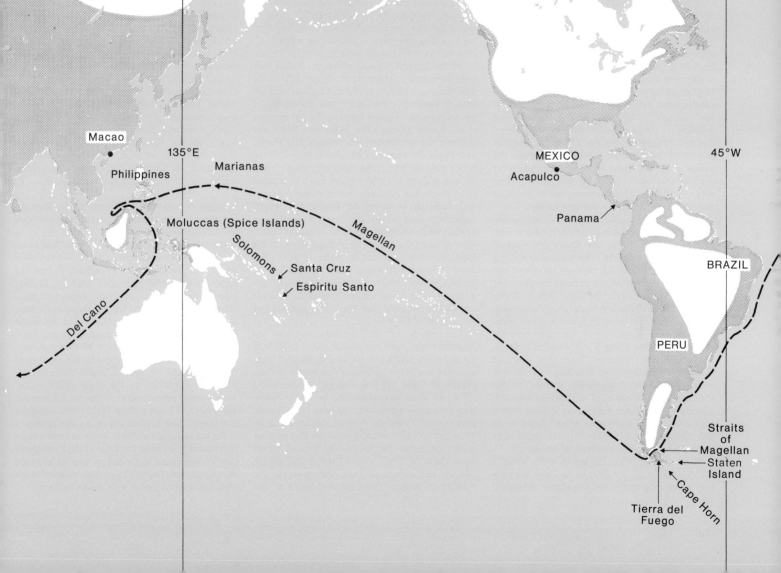

EXPLORATION OF THE PACIFIC 1521-1600

Macao

135°E

45°W

Philippines

Marianas

MEXICO

Acapulco

Moluccas (Spice Islands)

Magellan

Panama

Solomons

Santa Cruz

BRAZIL

Espiritu Santo

Del Cano

PERU

Straits
of
Magellan

Staten
Island

Cape Horn

Tierra del
Fuego

The World in 1600
3. Exploration in the North Atlantic and the New World to 1600

Until the end of the sixteenth century the routes to the East discovered by Vasco da Gama and Magellan were effectively monopolized by the Iberian powers: to the English and Dutch it seemed that their only hope of reaching oriental markets lay in the discovery of new routes in the northern hemisphere. The initial attempt was English, the idea being to sail along the northern edge of Asia. In 1553 the first part of this 'northeast passage' – the stage between London and Archangel – was successfully reconnoitred by Richard Chancellor. By the 1580s both English and Dutch had reached Novaya Zemlya and the mouth of the Ob. There they came up against the pack ice that was to defeat all attempts at further progress. By the 1620s it was clear to everyone that there was no viable north-east passage.

The north-west passage had a more exclusively English history, beginning with Frobisher's voyages to the mouths of the Davis and Hudson Straits in 1576–8. In 1587 Davis sailed up the first of these straits (which lies between Greenland and Baffin Land) as far as the edge of the pack ice. Interest then shifted to the other side of Baffin Land and in 1610 Hudson began a careful exploration of the bay that bears his name. A winter in the bay destroyed the morale of the expedition: the men mutinied and Hudson was set adrift never to be seen again. However, from the confused accounts of the survivors it looked as if the bay might be the much-hoped-for opening to the Pacific and a new series of expeditions followed. The most professional were led by William Baffin, who, after careful exploration of both Davis Strait and Hudson's Bay (1615–16), concluded that there was 'no passage, nor hope of passage'.

These voyages were failures in every sense – usable routes were not there to be found and little was added to geographical knowledge during the search. The Norse had done most of it before and, if some of what was found was news in Western Europe, it was nearly all old hat to the Icelanders and Russians. The only genuine discoveries were Hudson's Bay and Spitzbergen, the latter chanced upon during a wildly unrealistic Dutch phase in which the plan was to reach China by sailing over the Pole. The sole practical result of the whole business was an extension of whaling to polar waters.

All the Spanish voyages across the Pacific (bar one immediate successor of Magellan's) were mounted from Mexico or Peru. This was sensible enough logistically but meant that knowledge of the southern tip of South America did not increase at all. For all anyone knew Magellan's Strait was the only connection between Atlantic and Pacific and Tierra del Fuego could have stretched to the South Pole. In fact, many sixteenth-century maps showed it doing just that – there was a firm belief in an Australian continent that stretched from the real Australia to Tierra del Fuego. This belief, apparently inspired by the desire to make the world's land area balance the known area of ocean, even survived the discovery of Cape Horn by the Dutchmen Schouten and le Maire in 1616. Because they saw tiny Staten Island to their left on the way in they thought their discovery was simply a second strait. It was another generation before it was finally accepted that there was nothing but water south of Cape Horn.

The march of the *conquistadors* on the American mainland has already been described: the first phase which overran all major settled communities resulted in an empire that stretched from Mexico to Chile. The link with the colonies along the River Plate was established by 1548. Before then the southern continent had been crossed at its widest point. Francisco Pizarro, the conqueror of Peru, put his half-brother Gonzalo in charge of an expedition across the Andes. The column set off from Quito in 1541, crossed the Andes on the equator and descended from the snows to the Amazonian jungle. Three hundred miles of this reduced the Spaniards to despair. They had, however, found a sizable river (the Napo) and Gonzalo decided to send his second-in-command Orellana ahead by boat to see if there was any point in exploring further. Orellana was supposed to come back, but he kept going. Where the Napo joined a larger river some of the crew refused his orders and were put ashore. Gonzalo, struggling along through the jungle, eventually came up with these men and, learning of his lieutenant's desertion, turned the remains of his expedition about. While Gonzalo hacked his way back to the Andes, Orellana drifted eastward with the Amazon. Incredibly, both men made it – Orellana after a 2,000-mile journey that took him eighteen months. This epic was rivalled in 1560–61 by Aguirre's expedition down the Upper Amazon, up its Negro tributary and down the Orinoco. The main geographical features of South America had been filled in.

North America was a different matter. Here the big rivers ran in unhelpful directions: there were no Amerindian settlements of sufficient size to be worth conquering and consequently no firm bases for further exploration. However, rumours of cities paved with gold did elicit two expeditions from the second *conquistador* generation. De Soto, starting from Florida, ranged across the southern United States as far north as the Carolinas and as far west as Arkansas and Louisiana (1539–42). He found few Indians and no gold. Coronado, starting from Mexico, covered Arizona, New Mexico and parts of Texas and Kansas (1540–42). He discovered the only sizable villages in North America, the Pueblo communities of the upper Rio Grande. They were so poverty-stricken that the Spanish did not bother to occupy them until 1560, when the province of New Mexico was set up in this area.

On the east coast of North America there was no penetration at all apart from that of the Frenchman Cartier, who sailed up the St Lawrence as far as the site of Montreal (1536). The few English and French attempts at colonization were instant failures.

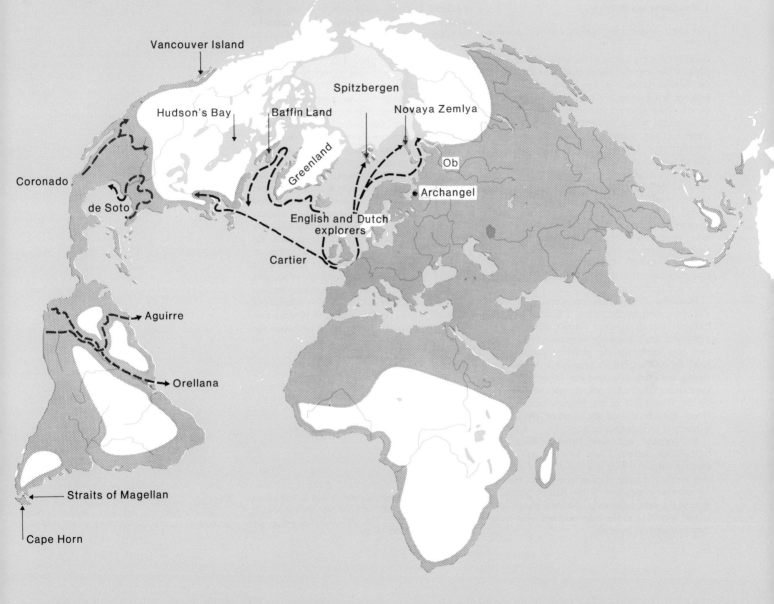

EXPLORATION IN THE NORTH ATLANTIC AND THE NEW WORLD TO **1600**

Vancouver Island

Spitzbergen

Hudson's Bay

Baffin Land

Novaya Zemlya

Greenland

Ob

Coronado

Archangel

de Soto

English and Dutch explorers

Cartier

Aguirre

Orellana

Straits of Magellan

Cape Horn

Europe in 1483
1. Population and Religion

Each symbol represents 1 million people, Catholic, Orthodox or Moslem

Because the early Christian hierarchy was an exact copy of the Imperial bureaucracy, the division of the Roman Empire in the fourth century A.D. resulted in a division of Christianity. Empires and churches had different fates. The Western Empire disintegrated within a century, leaving behind a western (Latin, Catholic) church that had been transformed willy-nilly into an autonomous, international organization. This had its bad moments but by and large prospered. The Eastern Empire survived the crisis that finished its Western counterpart: indeed, it survived so long that the eastern (Greek, Orthodox) church became politically identified with it. This handicapped Orthodox missionaries as against Catholic, the only important Orthodox converts being the Russians (and they set up a church of their own), whereas the Catholics converted the Scandinavians, Germans, Poles and Hungarians.

However, it was Islam, not Catholicism, that was responsible for Orthodoxy's final eclipse. The Catholic church survived Islam's attack almost unscathed: Spain and Sicily were lost and regained, only the North African province vanished for good. By contrast, Islam's progress in the East was steady, and eventually complete: the entire area of the Eastern Empire had passed under Moslem rule by the second half of the fifteenth century. The Greek church entered the modern era as the ministry of an oppressed minority.[1]

The contest was now between Islam and Catholicism, between a new East that was bigger than the old, and a West that was different in that it was purely European. The difference was critical, for whereas populations in the Islamic provinces were of the same order as in antiquity, populations in the West had at the least doubled. This more than balanced the equation.

The heartland of Europe – the zone of well-populated lands on either side of a line joining London and Rome – was not as yet threatened by the Islamic advance. The Ottomans would have to cross the Balkan glacis before reaching even its outer defences. But Islam had shown – in India for example – its ability to fight its way up population gradients. The distance between Upper and Lower Danube gave Europe time, not absolute security.

Just how impotent mere numbers could be was demonstrated by the nomads' domination of Russia. For centuries those masters of cavalry warfare, the Tartars of the Golden Horde, had terrorized ten times their number of peasants. It was a remarkable achievement but one that was entirely dependent on a single skill. With the advent of firearms, the superiority of mounted archer over foot-soldier vanished, and the military situation reversed. Of the khanates into which the Golden Horde divided, the south-western, the Khanate of Crimea, became an Ottoman protectorate, the north-eastern, the Khanate of Kazan, a vassal of Moscow. So long a source of terrible, irresistible armies, the steppe had suddenly become a power vacuum. So long the humble tributary of an Asiatic power, the Principality of Moscow now emerged as an active player in the European war game.

---

1. The Russian Orthodox church was in little better case, for half of its adherents had been incorporated in Catholic Poland when that state expanded east at the expense of the Golden Horde.

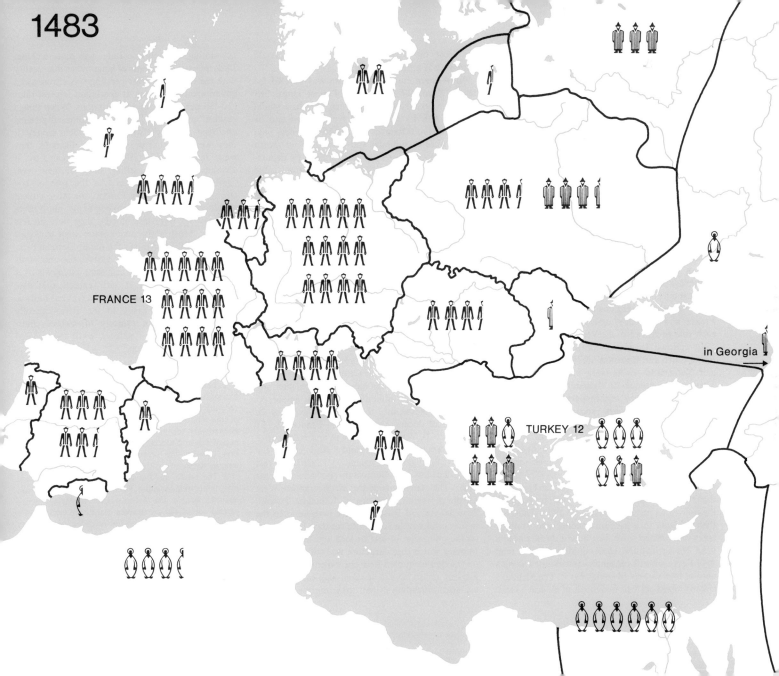

1483

FRANCE 13

TURKEY 12

in Georgia

Europe in 1483
2. Towns, Trade and Revenues

In the late fifteenth century only $2\frac{1}{2}$ per cent of Western Europeans lived in towns.[1] This low proportion reflects the overwhelmingly rural nature of pre-industrial society. However, being an average, the figure conceals the fact that two areas – the Netherlands and Northern Italy – had already reached the 10 per cent level and had an urban life of considerable vigour. This exceptionally high proportion of town-dwellers reflects their dominance of contemporary commerce and industry: the Netherlanders supplied the imports and controlled the exports of North European primary producers from the Baltic to Spain, the North Italians did the same for the agricultural areas of the Mediterranean (Spain, Southern Italy and the Islamic countries) besides carrying the spices and silks of the East on the last leg of their journey to Europe. The two systems were connected by routes across France and Germany, and Venetian ships sailed each year to Antwerp, the Venice of the North.[2]

In contrast to administrative capitals such as Paris, Cairo and Constantinople the North Italian and Netherland towns were creators of wealth. They were consequently tremendous assets to the states in which they lay. In particular they were every chancellor's ideal source of revenue – pockets of high income where wealth could be tapped in that best of all forms, cash. Western Europe, after the interlude of the Dark Ages, had returned to a money economy and cash was the crying need.

Thanks to their financial strength the biggest of the North Italian towns were able to maintain themselves as states in their own right. They ran their budgets in a modern manner and imposed taxes that yielded something near a ducat a head a year. No agricultural state could match this rate; only Egypt with its peasantry concentrated along a natural highway could come near it. The Mamluke sultans raised perhaps two thirds of a ducat a head:

the most the equally despotic Ottomans could manage was a third of a ducat.

In Western Europe despotism was beyond the reach, if not the aspiration, of most kings. For centuries their subjects had been used to a feudal society with its tithes fixed by tradition and its obligations discharged by service. Money payments were exceptional and made only in return for a review of grievances as expressed by deputations, parliaments or estates. In France and Castile the kings had gained the upper hand over these representatives partly because the long wars of liberation against the English and Moslems provided an impeccable pretext for taxation, more particularly because the nobles – the only really dangerous source of opposition – were exempted from the taxes they voted. In Castile they even got a cut of the proceeds. England, by contrast, accepted the new Tudor dynasty in 1486 only on condition that the king 'lived of his own', i.e. ran the country on the profits from his own estates plus the custom duties. The average Western European revenue was around a quarter of a ducat per head: the new English king's income was equivalent to less than one tenth of a ducat from each of his subjects.

As for total revenue the Ottoman and Mameluke exchequers received far larger amounts than any Western state – 4 million ducats a year apiece. At the end of the century the European sequence (in millions of ducats per year) was France (2·75), Castile (1·3), Venice (0·9), Milan and Naples (0·3 each), Aragon and Burgundy (0·5 each), the Papacy, Portugal and England (0·3 each). The rest had 0·2 or less. The German throne had no income at all. The states outside the Mediterranean–West European region – Hungary, Lithuania–Poland, Scandinavia and Russia – were peripheral to the money economy and depended for their functioning on the obligation of serf to lord and lord to king. In other words their structure was still feudal.

The figures quoted iron out violent annual fluctuations and so have to be taken with caution. They are also misleading in that they imply a grasp of

accounting that, outside Italy, was quite lacking. Budgets were statements of hope rather than reality with the result that overspending was chronic and government borrowing at exorbitant interest rates (10–30 per cent) almost continuous. When things reached crisis point kings had traditionally relied on fining the people who had lent them money (if they were Italians) or massacring them (if they were Jews), debasing the coinage (again) or, if absolutely cornered, selling some of their legal rights or personal estates. As the rule of law strengthened its grip on Europe, the more violent expedients became impossible to apply, but if royal bankruptcies were less bloody, they were no less frequent. Most of the major states went bankrupt every generation. Among the minor German principalities things were even worse: the enormous amounts involved in exceptional payments – a princess's dowry might well exceed the state revenue for a year – encouraged a feckless attitude that came all too easily to the aristocratically educated. Dozens of princely Micawbers entertained bailiffs in their palaces, while they waited for something to turn up.[3]

1. Defining a town as having not less than 30,000 inhabitants.

2. England was a pure primary producer till the mid fourteenth century, when she started to make up an increasing proportion of her wool into cloth. At the end of the fifteenth century the cloth still went to the Netherlands for finishing and distribution, so at this period England can be regarded as in process of transition between the primary producing and part-commercial states.

3. The astute could of course make money in seemingly impossible situations. For example, in 1514 a shrewd operator bought the Archbishopric of Mainz (which carried one of the seven votes cast at the election of a German Emperor) although the revenues were already entirely absorbed in paying the interest on the public debt. For the Archbishopric and for the right to sell indulgences he paid the Pope 40,000 ducats, which he almost entirely recovered from the sale of the indulgences. At the next Imperial election, that of Charles V four years later, he sold his vote for 90,000 ducats.

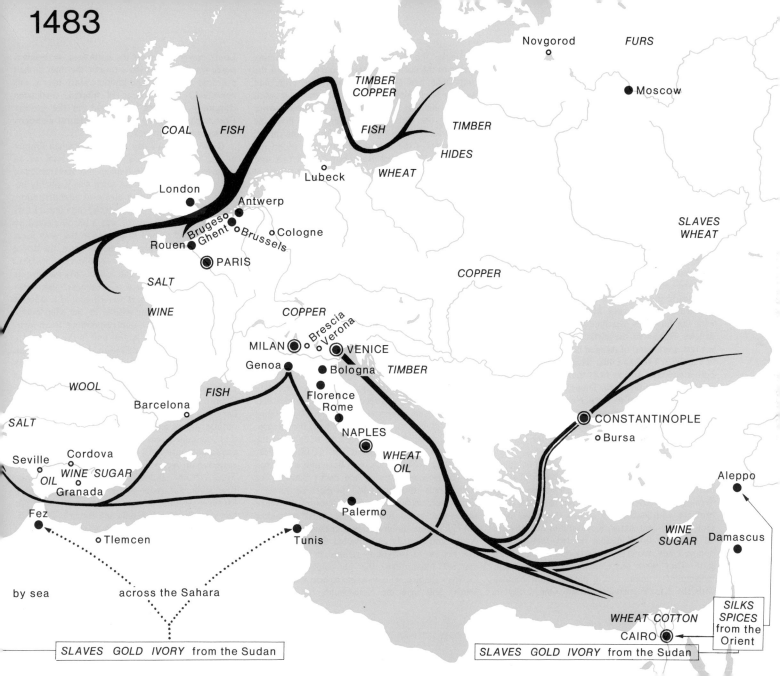

1483

FURS

Novgorod

Moscow

TIMBER
COPPER

COAL   FISH   FISH   TIMBER

HIDES

Lubeck

London   WHEAT

Antwerp
Bruges   Cologne   SLAVES
Ghent   Brussels   WHEAT

Rouen

PARIS

COPPER

SALT

WINE

COPPER

Brescia
Verona
MILAN   VENICE

Genoa   Bologna   TIMBER

WOOL   FISH   Florence
Rome

Barcelona   CONSTANTINOPLE
NAPLES
Bursa

SALT   WHEAT
OIL

Seville   Cordova   Aleppo
WINE SUGAR
OIL   Palermo   WINE
Granada   SUGAR   Damascus

Fez

Tlemcen   Tunis

by sea   across the Sahara   WHEAT COTTON
SILKS
SPICES
from the
Orient

SLAVES GOLD IVORY from the Sudan   CAIRO

SLAVES GOLD IVORY from the Sudan

The Middle Ages saw the creation of some but by no means all of the national units inherent in the geography and language structure of Western Europe. By the fifteenth century, Portugal, England and France were established political entities. Germany had the appearance of a state but had lost the substance. Italy remained a jigsaw. This uneven picture was to prove surprisingly long-lasting: the only addition to the number of nation-states right up to the nineteenth century being Spain, which emerged as a major power in the opening decades of the modern era.

In 1483 Spain still bore its medieval appearance. A Moslem state, the Emirate of Granada, survived in the south; the little Kingdom of Navarre maintained the independence of the Basques in the north; Castile held the bulk of the Peninsula; Aragon the Mediterranean seaboard with the Balearics, Sardinia and Sicily as dependencies. But under the surface things were changing fast. Ferdinand of Aragon had married Isabella of Castile in 1469 and their daughter would inherit both kingdoms. And in 1481 they had begun a war of attrition with Granada. Though every hamlet in the Emirate seemed to require a formal siege and there was little to show for the first years of campaigning, the outcome could hardly be in doubt. With the capture of Malaga in 1487 the job was half done.

In the medieval period France, which on paper was certainly Christendom's most powerful state, had tended to function below par. This was largely because the French kings were apt to endow their brothers with duchies of a size that gave them semi-independent status. Royal dukes not only ate up resources the Kingdom needed, they reflexly opposed any move towards a more centralized state. They were the champions of aristocratic indiscipline at home and, if pushed, collaborators with the King's enemies abroad. One duchy in

particular, the Duchy of Burgundy, was a standing threat to the security of the country. In 1384 the first Duke had acquired by marriage large and wealthy territories in the Netherlands. As a result the 'Burgundian state' became a European power pursuing its own policy. There was little the French King could do about it for, of the dukes' possessions – the Duchy of Burgundy (A on the map), the County of Burgundy (B), Artois and Picardy (C), Flanders (D), and the Central Netherlands (E) – only A, C and D were inside the French frontier. The dukes made skilful use of the English invasions of France to further their ambitions, deserting the English only when the French, beaten to the ground, temporarily recognized Burgundian independence. Linking the Netherlands with Burgundy proper was the next stage in the programme.

The man who solved the Burgundian problem was Louis XI, who came to the throne of France in 1461. Because he was both treacherous and successful, his admirers have called him Machiavellian, but his intellectual abilities were strictly limited, his natural impulsiveness poorly controlled and his qualities, good and bad, really those of a peasant. His strongest suit was tenacity, and the only modern quality of his otherwise credulous mind was a recognition that money was the measure of power. He taxed his subjects hard and spent the money fast. When the Anglo-Burgundian alliance re-formed he bought off the English (150,000 ducats down, 10,000 a year thereafter). When the Duke of Burgundy attempted the conquest of Lorraine (the duchy between the Netherlands and Burgundy proper) he hired a Swiss mercenary army which defeated the Duke twice and killed him at their third encounter (1477). Louis immediately annexed Burgundy, Artois and Picardy and invaded the Netherlands. The heiress to Burgundy refused to give in. She married Maximilian, the heir-apparent to the German Empire, who was able to beat back Louis' armies and save the Netherlands for his wife.

Louis, never lucky on the battlefield, accepted a peace on this basis. (In terms of the map he had acquired A, B and C and his suzerainty over D was conceded.) As a source of internal dissension Burgundy had been eliminated: in the process France had acquired the strong central authority she had previously lacked.[1]

By Maximilian's day the 'Holy Roman Empire of the German Nation' had failed both as an empire (over the North Italians and Slavs) and as a purely German Reich. Its scale was probably beyond the capacities of a medieval administration, but its decline into near-anarchy was ensured by the fact that the Emperor was a baron elected by his peers and so had to pander to the very force that disrupted so many medieval states, the desire of the barons for autonomy. No revenue attached to the Imperial throne and it was only because its possession was a source of weakness rather than strength that the electors were prepared to allow a monopoly of the succession to the Hapsburgs, whose family lands – corresponding to modern Austria – formed the largest unit in the empire.

The boundary of the Empire shown on the map is the official one. It includes North Italy, the Swiss confederation, the Burgundian Netherlands and Holstein (at the base of Denmark). In so far as the Empire meant anything in practical terms its boundary was not this legal one but the purely German outline shown on the next map of Europe. Even this contained close on 300 effectively self-governing states. All the sizable ones lay in the eastern half. Actually touching the eastern frontier were (from north to south) Pomerania, Brandenburg, Lusatia–Silesia (L and S on the map), Moravia (M) and, finally, Austria. Just inside this tier were Saxony, Bohemia and Bavaria. Bohemia, Moravia and Lusatia–Silesia formed a Slav enclave within an otherwise German area and were usually united politically. The Emperor was elected by the Archbishops of Mainz, Trier and Cologne and the rulers of Bohemia, Brandenburg, Saxony and the Palatinate (which is the two-part state with one half

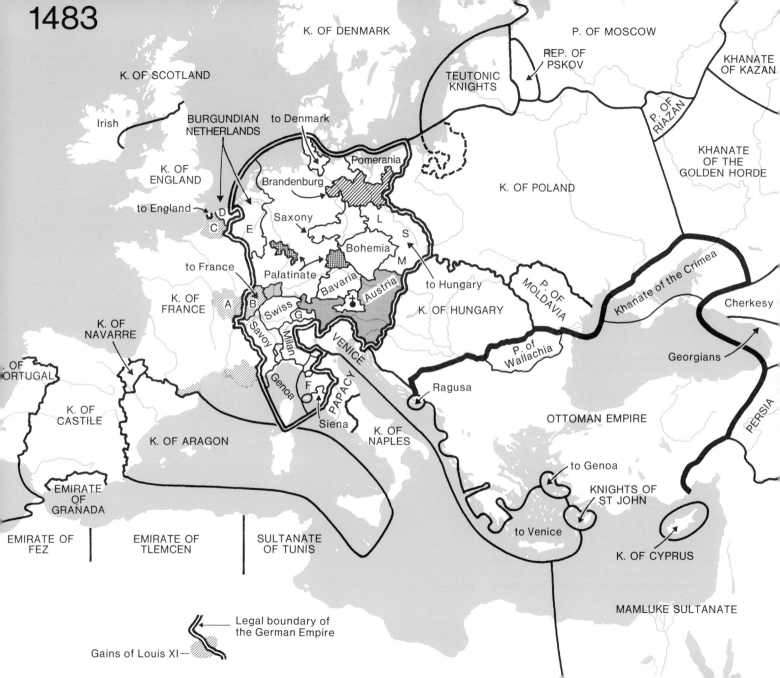

1483

K. OF DENMARK

P. OF MOSCOW

K. OF SCOTLAND

REP. OF PSKOV

KHANATE OF KAZAN

TEUTONIC KNIGHTS

Irish

BURGUNDIAN NETHERLANDS

to Denmark

P. OF RIAZAN

KHANATE OF THE GOLDEN HORDE

Pomerania

K. OF ENGLAND

Brandenburg

K. OF POLAND

to England

D

Saxony

L

C

E

S

to France

Bohemia

M

Palatinate

Bavaria

Austria

Khanate of the Crimea

Cherkesy

K. OF FRANCE

A B

Swiss

G

to Hungary

P. OF MOLDAVIA

K. OF NAVARRE

Savoy

Milan

VENICE

K. OF HUNGARY

Genoa

F

PAPACY

P. of Wallachia

Georgians

OF ORTUGAL

Siena

Ragusa

K. OF CASTILE

K. OF NAPLES

OTTOMAN EMPIRE

PERSIA

EMIRATE OF GRANADA

K. OF ARAGON

to Genoa

EMIRATE OF FEZ

EMIRATE OF TLEMCEN

SULTANATE OF TUNIS

KNIGHTS OF ST JOHN

to Venice

K. OF CYPRUS

MAMLUKE SULTANATE

Legal boundary of the German Empire

Gains of Louis XI

of the Middle Rhine, one half in the angle between Bohemia and Bavaria).

Despite the Imperial crown Hapsburg fortunes were currently at a very low ebb. Earlier in the century they had flown high, with a shrewd marriage that had netted the Kingdom of Bohemia (plus Moravia and Lusatia–Silesia) and the Kingdom of Hungary. Alas, the natives had not taken too kindly to German rule and in 1459 the elective element in their monarchies had enabled them to kick the Hapsburg habit. The Hungarians voted in one of their own nobles, the Bohemians did the same, then, when their first choice died, offered the throne to the Crown Prince of Poland. In the resulting three-cornered struggle between Hapsburgs, Hungarians and Poles, the Hungarians definitely came out on top, taking Moravia and Silesia from the Bohemian–Polish forces and in 1485 a good slice of Austria from the Hapsburgs.

Several minor enclaves in Germany require a note. The two small Hapsburg areas on either side of the Upper Rhine are, on the left bank, Upper Alsace (Sundgau) and, on the right bank, Upper Baden (Breisgau). Between Austria and Bavaria is the independent bishopric of Salzburg (marked with an orb). In the angle between Switzerland, Austria and Milan is the Confederation of the Grisons (marked G), shortly to be absorbed by the Swiss (1497).

The Italian jigsaw also needs itemizing. Venice and, to a much lesser extent, Genoa were wealthy and important because they were the channels through which the products of the Levant and Far East reached Europe. Though they were of little account by land, their navies ruled the Mediterranean (Genoa definitely in second place; Aragon would be third) and in the Adriatic and Levant Venice held a string of bases left over from the Crusades. Milan and Florence (F) were also rich little states as a result of their manufactures and because of the more developed level of Italian capitalism as compared with the rest of Europe. However, neither could field a serious army. Savoy

and the minor states north and south of Florence were of no importance, the Papal State equally impotent in temporal terms as it had little effective control outside Rome. Southern Italy, conquered by Aragon in 1442, but ruled as an independent kingdom by an illegitimate branch of the Aragonese house, was Italy's largest state. The story goes that Lorenzo the Magnificent of Florence by his diplomatic skill kept the balance of power in the peninsula: in military terms it was the lack of power that maintained the balance.

Moving east, countries become bigger but people thinner on the ground (which is why the larger states of Germany lie along its eastern border). Poland was a feudal state with an elective monarchy, almost as devoid of a central authority as Germany. In the Middle Ages it had lost its Baltic seaboard to the Teutonic Knights and appeared to be doomed to a servile role on the fringe of Christendom. The Lithuanians to the north proved tougher: they held off the Teutonic Knights (and a similar outfit, the Livonian Knights, which had conquered Estonia and Latvia) and then took advantage of the decline of the Golden Horde to make themselves masters of all Central Russia. The union of Poland and Lithuania created a power strong enough to turn the tables on the Teutonic Knights (who had absorbed the Livonian order in 1237). The first Polish victory came at Tannenburg in 1411. After a second, fifty years later, the Knights were forced to disgorge much of their territory and pay homage for the Prussian lands that they retained.

1. Louis also bought the bit of Aragon that lay north of the Pyrenees (for 300,000 ducats) and inherited Provence.

Problems of nomenclature:
the Netherlands and Savoy

In this atlas the Netherlands means the triangular area bounded by the North Sea and the modern frontiers of France and Germany. At various times various parts have been termed Burgundian, Spanish and Austrian – these terms denoting political control by non-Netherland powers. The intrinsic division is into north and south. The north part of the Netherlands has evolved into the Netherlands of today: its inhabitants are the Dutch. In the past the Dutch state has been known as the United Provinces, the Dutch Republic or Holland, and its people have been termed Hollanders or Flemings. I use the term Holland only in its strict meaning of Amsterdam province and Flemish in the modern fashion to mean the Dutch-speaking inhabitants of the Southern Netherlands.

The southern part of the Netherlands has evolved into Belgium. The situation here was (and is) more complicated because the area is half Flemish (Dutch-speaking), half French-speaking. Coveted by France, defended by the Spanish, Dutch, Germans and English, it became 'the cockpit of Europe', a status it lost only with the general recognition of its independence in the mid nineteenth century. Understandably, it has identity problems. The word 'Belgium' is itself a consciously neutral borrowing from the Roman period when a Celtic tribe called the Belgae inhabited the area.

Savoy, another fifteenth-century frontier state, has now been partitioned between France and Italy. The state took its name from the province of Savoy on the French side of the Alps, its main resources were in Piedmont on the Italian side. To distinguish the provinces I have used the terms 'transalpine' and 'cisalpine'. 'Cis' means 'this side of', 'trans' 'beyond'. The terms, being Roman in origin, are used from the Roman point of view. (Exceptions to this rule are Transcaucasia which is from the viewpoint of Moscow and Transylvania, which is 'beyond the woods' from Hungary.)

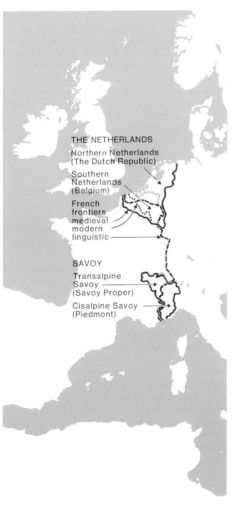

THE NETHERLANDS

Northern Netherlands
(The Dutch Republic)

Southern
Netherlands
(Belgium)

French
frontiers
medieval
modern
linguistic

SAVOY

Transalpine
Savoy
(Savoy Proper)

Cisalpine Savoy
(Piedmont)

Europe in 1520
Political Units

Firmly established on the Lower Danube at the beginning of the fifteenth century, the Ottomans were no further forward at the beginning of the sixteenth. Initially this lack of progress was due to the need to mop up Christian enclaves to the south; Mahomet II (1451–81) not only had to conquer Constantinople but various other Byzantine and Crusader remnants in the Balkans. Latterly it was the ineffectual personality of Mahomet's son Bayezid II (1481–1512) that was to blame. Bayezid did a little more mopping-up – in particular he took all but two of the Venetian fortresses in mainland Greece – but for most of his reign he did nothing at all. In the east both the Mamlukes and Persians were hostile, and in case trouble might break out elsewhere Bayezid refused to commit himself in any direction. The Ottoman state, being a military machine, eventually proved unable to tolerate this indecision; an army revolt put Bayezid's son Selim the Grim on the throne and he set the machine in motion again.

Selim decided to settle with his Moslem rivals first. Four victorious campaigns in four years showed that Ottoman arms had lost none of their edge. The Persians were swept out of Eastern Turkey and Northern Mesopotamia in 1514–15. One Mamluke Sultan was killed while unsuccessfully defending Syria against Selim's invasion of 1516, the next (and last) Sultan was captured and executed when Egypt itself fell to the Ottoman forces the following year. Master of the whole Near East, Selim died in 1520. The first act of his successor Suleiman was to clear the European frontier for action by eliminating the Hungarian bridgehead at Belgrade (1521).

At the other end of the Mediterranean it was the Christians who were on the offensive. Ferdinand and Isabella finally reduced Granada in 1492. The crusading spirit was revived by this overdue success and a full-scale invasion of North Africa seemed on the cards. It would have been a pretty profitless operation and Ferdinand was never keen, but the unexpectedly easy success of the first Spanish attacks encouraged him to try for control of the coastline. In this he was largely successful – by 1510 most of the major ports had fallen to seaborne assault[1] – but while the hinterland remained hostile it was a fragile achievement. With the resources and manpower of Spain increasingly diverted to the attractive opportunities on offer in Italy and the New World, the chance of Spanish armies ever campaigning in the interior faded.

In 1483 Charles VIII inherited a strong France and a weak claim to the throne of Naples. The better claim was held by Ferdinand, but Charles hoped to buy him off by ceding the frontier province of Aragon that Louis XI had purchased from Ferdinand's father. Charles also thought he could satisfy Maximilian's claim to the full Burgundian inheritance by acquiescing in Maximilian's re-occupation of Artois, Picardy and the County of Burgundy. These entirely practical gains of Louis XI were thrown away so that Charles could march to Naples and back again (1494–5), Ferdinand making sure that the French garrison was expelled as soon as Charles had left. In 1498 Charles hit his big stupid head on a lintel at Fontainebleau and died, to be succeeded by Louis XII, who had a small head and a claim to Milan as well as Naples.

A slightly less foolish invasion of Italy followed which resulted in a French occupation of Milan (1499) and, a year later, an agreed partition of Naples between Ferdinand and Louis. The allies soon quarrelled (they had intended to from the start). The resulting war, which mixed battle and tourney in a last flourish of the medieval style, ended in complete victory for Spain's 'gran capitano', Gonzales da Cordoba. Ferdinand added the crown of Naples to his collection and the scene of conflict moved north. The Pope, the Swiss, Venice and Ferdinand formed a coalition to expel the French from the Peninsula, an object they achieved in 1512. In the same year direct warfare

with France across the Pyrenees gave Ferdinand the opportunity to annex Navarre.

The discovery and proclaimed monopoly of the New World (see p. 16), the assumption of the offensive lead in Christendom's war with the infidel, the succession of victories in Italy over the best armies France could field, all make Spain's debut in international affairs as astonishing in retrospect as it was to contemporaries. At a time when she was still unaware of her own unity, Spain had leapt to a position in Europe that rivalled France's centuries old pre-eminence. Fortune smiled on Spanish arms but Ferdinand deserves his traditional share of the credit. Ever willing to compromise, always offering to take the smaller half, he usually ended up with the whole bag.

Ferdinand and Isabella's sole surviving child was a daughter, Joanna. She had married Philip, Maximilian's son by his Burgundian wife. Philip died while still a young man: Joanna used the occasion for behaviour of spectacular lunacy and had to be declared incompetent; their combined possessions passed to their eldest child, Charles. This fabulous inheritance – the Netherlands, the Hapsburg lands in Germany, the Spanish kingdoms with their dependencies in the Mediterranean and the New World – made Charles seem a reincarnation of Charlemagne and the arbiter of Western Christendom. Yet the age when Christendom was a meaningful idea was ending and even in face of Turkish aggression Charles was never able to achieve a European concert. The nation state was the unit of significance and in these terms Charles was simply a King of Spain with interests opposed to those of France in the German and Italian power vacuums. And France was on the offensive again. The year Charles came of age (1515) the French crowned a dashing new King, Francis I. He immediately led a French army over the Alps, won a decisive victory over the Swiss in a two-day battle at Marignano and reoccupied Milan.[2] Francis also challenged Charles in the German election that followed

Maximilian's death. By paying out 850,000 ducats in bribes Charles won the Imperial crown. In 1521 his army in North Italy once again expelled the French from Milan. The same year he ceded the Hapsburg possessions in Eastern Germany – and the problem of facing any Ottoman threat that might develop – to his brother Ferdinand. His own resources were fully committed to the task of safeguarding Italy and Western Germany from the French.

The opening decades of the sixteenth century were good years for Moscow. Various border towns were taken from Poland (particularly Chernigov in 1500 and Smolensk in 1514). Pskov was annexed in 1510. The Golden Horde disintegrated in 1502.

1. The exception is Algiers, which the Spaniards took but immediately lost in 1516. (They held on to a fortified island in the harbour till 1525.) Putting backbone into Moslem resistance in the town were the Barbarossa brothers, who carried the Ottoman Sultan's commission. They subsequently made Algiers the centre of an effective sea and land power acknowledging Turkish suzerainty. The Barbarossas were not, as is often said, Christian renegades but the sons of a janissary. The janissaries, the elite troops of the Ottoman army, were conscripted as children from the Christian community subject to the Ottomans and brought up by the state as Moslems and soldiers.

2. This was the end of the Swiss interlude in European military history. Since they had overthrown the last Duke of Burgundy Swiss pikemen had been considered unbeatable and a necessary (mercenary) component of all European armies. The Swiss did not often act on their own behalf, but their various interventions in Italy did result in an advance of their southern frontier which Francis was sensible enough to respect.

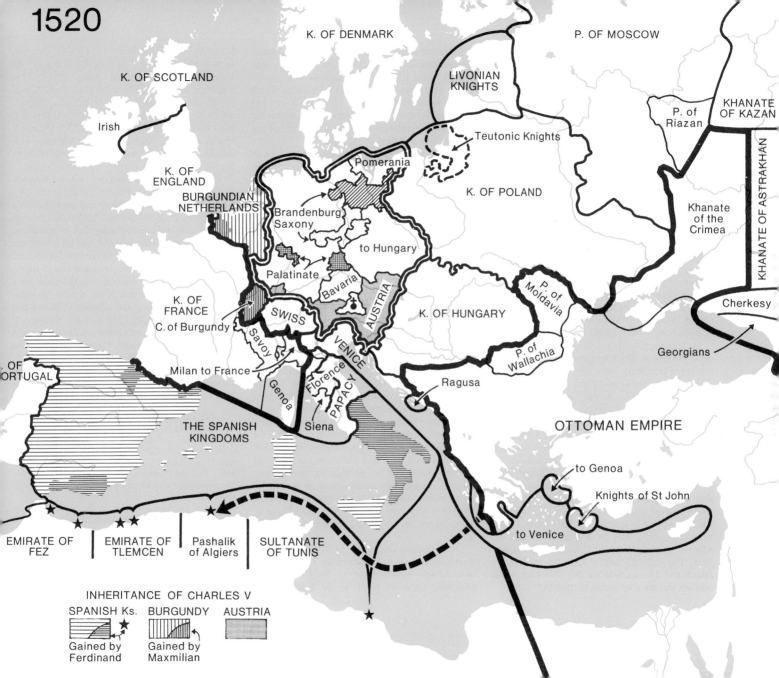

1520

K. OF DENMARK

K. OF SCOTLAND

P. OF MOSCOW

Irish

LIVONIAN KNIGHTS

P. of Riazan

KHANATE OF KAZAN

Teutonic Knights

K. OF ENGLAND

BURGUNDIAN NETHERLANDS

Pomerania

K. OF POLAND

Khanate of the Crimea

KHANATE OF ASTRAKHAN

Brandenburg

Saxony

to Hungary

Palatinate

Bavaria

AUSTRIA

K. OF FRANCE

C. of Burgundy

SWISS

Savoy

VENICE

K. OF HUNGARY

P. of Moldavia

Cherkesy

Milan to France

Genoa

Florence

PAPACY

Georgians

OF ORTUGAL

Siena

THE SPANISH KINGDOMS

P. of Wallachia

Ragusa

OTTOMAN EMPIRE

to Genoa

Knights of St John

to Venice

EMIRATE OF FEZ

EMIRATE OF TLEMCEN

Pashalik of Algiers

SULTANATE OF TUNIS

INHERITANCE OF CHARLES V

SPANISH Ks.   BURGUNDY   AUSTRIA

Gained by Ferdinand

Gained by Maxmilian

Europe in 1559
Political Units

Charles V got off to a good start. His French rival Francis I, who had more dash than brains, let his legal rights dictate his strategy and opted for another invasion of Italy (1524). Bar Spain, Italy was Charles's strongest point. At the battle of Pavia, Charles's army all but annihilated the French and Francis himself was taken prisoner (1525). Charles extorted a ransom of 2 million ducats and a highly favourable treaty, but Francis refused to give up the struggle – or even move it to more favourable ground. He repudiated the treaty (and stopped payment of the ransom) as soon as he was free. By 1528 his troops were again in Milan and even marching on Naples. But at the end of this year Charles persuaded Genoa to desert the French, leaving them without the sea-power to maintain themselves in the peninsula. Milan's uncertain status was only finally resolved when it was annexed to Spain in 1535, but Italy (except Venice and Savoy) was effectively under Spanish control from 1530.

In Germany Charles's position was and remained more precarious. The Hapsburg lands (delegated to brother Ferdinand) were only capable of self-defence, the Imperial power was merely titular and what unity remained to the German Reich was threatened by the religious upheaval whose political expression was the League of Protestant Princes. After some touch-and-go campaigning Charles managed to defeat the League and preserve his legal authority; he also maintained the Burgundian inheritance against French assaults. Though these were defensive victories they represent a considerable achievement, particularly as the French had finally realized that Germany was the Hapsburg soft spot. In contrast to conquests in Italy which, even if successful, could only be a drain on French resources, gains here would strengthen the French state. The strategic factors were all in France's favour and Charles held the line only because his soldiers had the edge on the battlefield.[1]

In his role as crusader Charles was less successful. He took Tunis in 1535 but failed ignominiously in an attempt on the Barbarossa stronghold of Algiers in 1541. Thereafter the Christian position in North Africa crumbled. By the mid-1550s the Turks had established control over the hinterland as well as the coast of Algeria and the few Spanish forts remaining were of little practical significance.

While Charles kept up the Hapsburg position in the world brother Ferdinand minded the home farm to good effect. The Hungarian Kingdom had been inherited by the King of Bohemia in 1490, producing an appetizing bloc of territory to which the Hapsburgs had a fair legal claim if the King died childless. The long expected Turkish invasion of Hungary ensured that he did – he was among the slain at the overwhelming Turkish victory of Mohacs (1526). Ferdinand swung into action brandishing his legal rights, proclaiming the need for unity in face of the Turk and promising the barons bribes of spectacular size. Bohemia (plus Moravia and Silesia) voted for him but the Hungarians again preferred a baron of their own. The Turks supported the local man and chased Ferdinand out of Hungary. It looked as though Ferdinand would have to be content with half the prize, but in the end sheer tenacity brought him a slice of Hungary too. He rode out the Turkish invasions of Austria in 1529 and 1532 and though he could not field an army to match the Ottoman he could usually beat the Hungarians when the Sultan's back was turned. After a generation of warfare the wreck of the Hungarian state was tacitly divided, Ferdinand getting the west and north, the Sultan the Danube valley and his protégé the east (Transylvania). Ferdinand's performance in defence of Christendom impressed the German princes. When Charles V abdicated in favour of his son Philip II, they insisted on Ferdinand getting the Imperial title.

Ottoman expansion in this period has been mentioned so far only as it affected the Hapsburgs, an unreasonable approach to an empire that was advancing on every front. In the long reign of Suleiman the Magnificent (1520–66) Ottoman armies reached as far as Algeria, Hungary, the Persian Gulf (1535) and Aden (1547). The Venetians lost their last foothold in mainland Greece (1540: they still held the islands, including Cyprus, which they had annexed in 1489); the Knights of St John were expelled from Rhodes (1522: Charles V resettled them in Malta). Suleiman's armies were rebuffed – notably at Vienna in 1529 and in Malta by the Knights in 1565 – but they were never beaten.

The Reformation finished the Teutonic Knights. In 1525 the Teutonic Master declared himself a Lutheran, dissolved the Order and made his fief a straightforward Polish duchy. This left the Livonian Knights, who had re-established their independence of the Teutonic Order in 1513, out on a limb and temptingly vulnerable. In 1558 Ivan the Terrible, the first Prince of Moscow to call himself Tsar of All the Russias, decided that Livonia was the place for a Western conquest to match his almost bloodless advances in the East – the Khanate of Kazan had fallen to his forces in 1552 and the Khanate of Astrakhan in 1556. Ivan's armies had an easy time in the first years but Poland, Denmark and Sweden (which had repudiated Danish rule in 1523) quickly discovered an equal interest in Livonia and as the various liberating forces converged on the province Ivan's move began to seem less shrewd.

1. The war only finally came to end with the Treaty of Cateau-Cambrésis in 1559, four years after Charles's abdication and two after a major Spanish victory at St Quentin, on the Netherlands border. France obtained the right to garrison bridgeheads across the upper Moselle (at Metz, Toul and Verdun): she also gained Saluzzo from Savoy and kept Calais which she had taken from the English the year before.

Charles rearranged several of the minor states of Germany and Italy. Saxony had been divided since 1485: the senior line backed the Protestant rising against Charles so he recast the division and transferred the electorate to the junior line in 1547. Florence got Siena in 1551 and the principality of Parma (P on the map) was carved out of Milan as a reward for papal co-operation (the Pope kept it in his family so it did not become part of the Papal State).

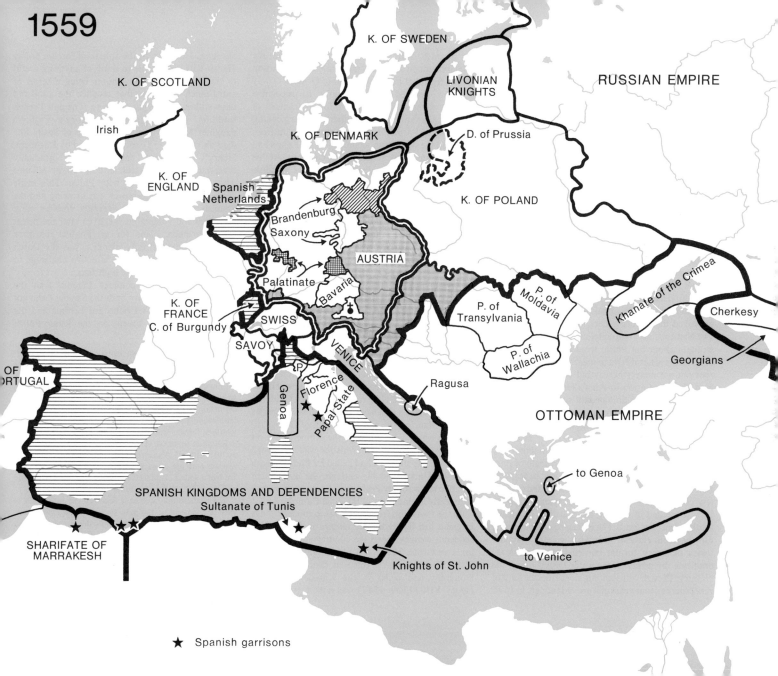

1559

K. OF SCOTLAND

Irish

K. OF ENGLAND

K. OF SWEDEN

LIVONIAN KNIGHTS

RUSSIAN EMPIRE

K. OF DENMARK

D. of Prussia

K. OF POLAND

Spanish Netherlands

Brandenburg

Saxony

AUSTRIA

Palatinate

Bavaria

K. OF FRANCE
C. of Burgundy

SWISS

SAVOY

VENICE

Genoa

P

Florence

Papal State

P. of Moldavia

P. of Transylvania

P. of Wallachia

Ragusa

Khanate of the Crimea

Cherkesy

Georgians

OTTOMAN EMPIRE

to Genoa

K. OF PORTUGAL

SPANISH KINGDOMS AND DEPENDENCIES
Sultanate of Tunis

Knights of St. John

to Venice

SHARIFATE OF MARRAKESH

★ Spanish garrisons

Europe in 1600
1. Political Units

Both Spain and France were exhausted when the Treaty of Cateau-Cambrésis was signed, and internal 'wars of religion' kept France flat on her back for the rest of the century. The three sickly grandsons of Francis I who reigned in turn over the French between 1559 and 1589 faced a difficult but by no means impossible situation: the Huguenot (Protestant) minority was a small one which a strong state could have dealt with firmly. As it was, the monarchy lied itself into compromises that outraged Catholic opinion and into massacres that horrified the Protestant world. Though the King gave the order for St Bartholomew's Eve (the massacre of the Huguenots in Paris in 1572) this was not an act of government but of abdication. The mob ruled the streets and faction ruled the country.

Philip II had an equally unhappy time. In 1566 his high-handedness in dealing with Protestants provoked the Netherlanders to civil disobedience. The Netherlanders had constitutional rights they felt strongly about but Philip would not negotiate: he ordered his general Alva to march up from Italy and root out not merely heresy but the liberties of the land. This was a job to Alva's taste: the terror he instituted quickly eliminated all sign of opposition. The rebels fled to England or Germany and, being seafarers, continued the struggle (and kept themselves alive) in the only way possible – attacking Spanish shipping in the Channel. Philip, apparently master of the situation, pressured Elizabeth of England into expelling them from her ports; in desperation the 'beggars of the sea' sailed home and seized a few coastal towns (1572). To everyone's surprise they succeeded in rallying the maritime provinces (Holland and Zeeland). The war against Spanish rule now began in earnest, with Alva winning easy victories on every formal battlefield but unable to eradicate the rebels on the water-logged rim of the country. Though withstanding sieges was the limit of rebel success, four years of it proved enough. In 1576

the Spanish administration went bankrupt, the soldiers went on strike and the whole country swung behind the rebel leader, William of Orange.

Philip spurned Orange's offer to recognize Spanish sovereignty in return for guarantees of religious toleration and civil liberty: a new general, the Duke of Parma, brought a new army up from Italy and the war began again. By 1586 Parma had pushed Orange almost back to the coastline. At this point Philip fatally widened the area of conflict. Because Protestant Elizabeth had been aiding the rebels, Parma was told to prepare to invade England. Spain's Atlantic fleet had been built up to unprecedented strength for the enterprise. The summer of 1588 found Parma waiting at Dunkirk for the much touted armada that was to ferry him across the straits. In the event, the armada fought its way up the Channel well enough but was then swept through to the North Sea by the weather and the English. Battered by both, it escaped home only by sailing round the British Isles – leaving its wrecks on every coast.

Philip's next idea (1590) was for Parma to intervene in France. Here Henry IV, though a Huguenot, was on the verge of succeeding in his claim to the French throne, left vacant by the extinction of the Valois line. The intervention was ineffective: Henry became undisputed King (and also turned Catholic) in 1594. Parma's absence from the Low Countries allowed Maurice, the son of William of Orange, to take the whole area north of the Rhine and a bit more besides. Though an armistice was not signed until 1607 the situation had gelled by Philip's death in 1598. Understandably enough, the new Dutch republic was strongly Protestant; its creation was the only really lasting work of the most Catholic King.[1]

In the transition from medieval to modern times England lost its traditional empire in France: the sixteenth century found the country still searching for a new role. Henry VII (1485–1509), founder of the Tudor dynasty, restored confidence in the monarchy and order in the Kingdom; his son Henry VIII (1509–1547) was able to rule as an

autocrat. However, in the sphere of foreign policy Henry VIII was unable to think of anything useful to do, his only positive actions being a series of anti-French flourishes that recalled the good old days without achieving anything. The anti-French tradition was continued by Henry's Catholic daughter Mary, who married Philip of Spain. She died childless (1558), to be suceeded by Elizabeth, Henry's Protestant daughter, who gradually reversed Mary's policies, ending up in alliance with France and at war with Philip. This made sense, for English sea-power was growing and the Spanish and Portuguese overseas empires were both rich and vulnerable. Yet even after the defeat of the armada, plans for an English maritime dominion remained only plans; it was the Dutch who were to make the first effective challenge to Spain and Portugal on the high seas.[2]

In his attempt to conquer Livonia Ivan the Terrible was defeated by both the Swedes (who got Estonia) and the Poles (who got Livonia and the restitution of some towns on the Russo-Polish frontier).

1. Philip didn't do much better in his more straightforward crusades. When the Turks invaded Cyprus he organized a relief fleet which won the handsome victory of Lepanto (1571). However, Cyprus had fallen ten weeks before the battle, which was without practical result. In 1574 Tunis was lost for good and four years later dreams of conquest in the interior of North Africa vanished forever when the Portuguese King Sebastian led a full-scale invasion of Morocco to catastrophic defeat at the battle of Alcazarquivir. Ironically this Christian disaster was the cause of Philip's sole political success. He had a sound claim to the throne of the dead Sebastian and by 1580 had made it good.

2. Elizabeth may not have foreseen the future but at least she cleaned up the past. One of the legacies of the traditional enmity with France was the Franco-Scottish alliance. Elizabeth subsidized the Protestant party in Scotland to such good effect that it gained permanent control and by dying childless she completed the good work, for the King of Scotland was her heir (1603). By the end of her reign Elizabeth had also made English rule fairly effective throughout Ireland.

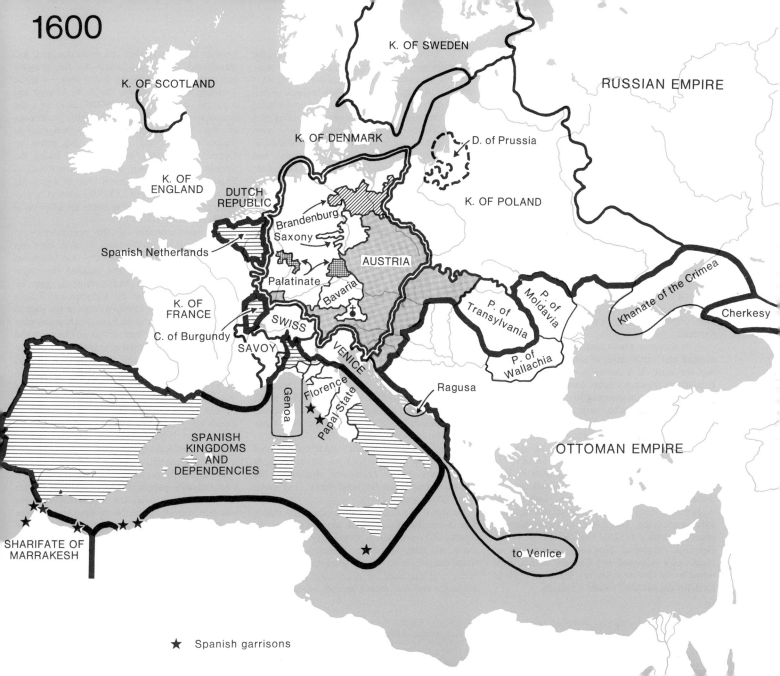

1600

K. OF SWEDEN

K. OF SCOTLAND

RUSSIAN EMPIRE

K. OF DENMARK

D. of Prussia

K. OF ENGLAND

DUTCH REPUBLIC

K. OF POLAND

Brandenburg

Saxony

AUSTRIA

Spanish Netherlands

Palatinate

Bavaria

P. of Transylvania

P. of Moldavia

Khanate of the Crimea

Cherkesy

K. OF FRANCE

C. of Burgundy

SWISS

SAVOY

VENICE

P. of Wallachia

Ragusa

Genoa

Florence

Papal State

SPANISH KINGDOMS AND DEPENDENCIES

OTTOMAN EMPIRE

to Venice

SHARIFATE OF MARRAKESH

★ Spanish garrisons

Each symbol represents 1 million people, Catholic, Protestant, Orthodox or Moslem

Man is a guilty animal, given to repentance and self-punishment; one of the most important reassurances offered to a Christian is that true repentance will be rewarded by God's forgiveness. From its beginnings the church had taken into consideration not only the apparent sincerity of the reformed sinner but such objective evidence of his repentance as pilgrimages, donations of money in lieu of pilgrimages and other donations of money. This was reasonable provided that gesture and emotion were not equated, but in the fifteenth century the church's growing need for cash led to an increasingly brisk attitude towards the sale of 'indulgences'. These spiritual pardons could be obtained (at a price) for any sin committed by any person, living or dead; sales were entrusted to papal legates specially selected for their persuasiveness.

In its economic aspect credulity is like any other demand and has its level of satisfaction: to maintain the value of a currency equivalent such as indulgences requires a sober hand on the printing press. Neither point occurred to the officials of the Papal Exchequer, who understandably enough wanted more and more sales. The Reformation began when German ecclesiastical credit collapsed as a result of a record-breaking tour by the Dominican friar Tetzel (1515–17) on behalf of the Archbishop of Mainz (see p. 24, footnote 3). Disillusioned Germans turned from Tetzel and his desperate promises to Martin Luther, an Augustinian monk whose intellectual doubts about indulgences soon progressed to repudiation of papal supremacy (1520). The nationalism of the Germans, frustrated politically, surged up in favour of a reformed and German church. Protected by the Elector of Saxony, Luther was able to establish the nuclear Protestant religion.

The breakdown of Catholicism's traditional monopoly was followed by the emergence of other forms of heterodoxy. Throughout the Middle Ages the downtrodden masses had been inclined to millennial outbursts in which despair fathered a belief in the imminence of Christ's second coming plus an indifference to personal property or – even more alarming – a feeling that property should be held in common. Unsurprisingly there was a bad outbreak (in south-west Germany) in 1524. Luther quickly disassociated himself from the rebels and from the Anabaptist sect which provided their fundamentalist tenets. Disassociated is too weak a word: the vehemence of his polemic 'Against the murdering, thieving hordes of peasants' does more credit to his realism than his humanity. But these revolts were always suppressed and Luther was determined to create an active, progressive church. He succeeded, while the peasants were massacred (as were all Anabaptists in all countries to the end of the century). When a successful left-wing group did appear within the reforming movement, far from being anarchist, it exaggerated Lutheran sobriety. Where Luther had attacked the corruption and excess dogma of Catholicism, the Frenchman Calvin addressed himself to the corruption and loose thinking of the individual. The near-theocracy he established at Geneva (1541) lasted only his lifetime, but the rigour of his views and the social discipline he demanded appealed to those who felt strongly enough about the Reformation to fight for it. While Calvinism made only limited headway in the comparatively tolerant atmosphere of Germany, to the persecuted Huguenots, the embattled Dutch and the rebel Scots, God spoke with Calvin's voice.

Germany was tolerant only in the sense that it was politically divided and anyone (except an Anabaptist) could find a principality whose ruler shared his faith. Apart from theological innovations, the reforming religion attracted the princes because it liquidated an organization that owed allegiance and sent money abroad, replaced it by another that was smaller and more obedient, and transferred the excess assets to the princely treasury. Consequently, the initial progress of the Lutheran reformation was rapid. By 1540 it had won the north-eastern third of Germany, the Scandinavian Kingdoms and the Baltic possessions of the Teutonic and Livonian Knights. In Switzerland and the remaining two thirds of Germany (excluding the Hapsburg lands) the reformers also did well; and once Henry VIII of England had declared himself head of a national church (which he did in 1534) the attempt to give this a genuine identity had to end in the adoption of a reformed faith.

The last successes of the reformers – in Scotland and the Netherlands – came later and more bloodily. They were the last successes because the wave had now reached the major powers, whose rulers had nothing to gain by espousing the cause of the Reformation. France and Spain had been strong enough in the past to force concessions from the Papacy. Their churches were already more or less national in character and paid a proportion of their revenues to the secular exchequer. Hapsburg and Valois held to the old faith and when a Huguenot Bourbon succeeded to the French throne, his conversion to Catholicism was dictated by the interests of the Kingdom. By the end of the century the Papacy had regained confidence and proclaimed the counter-Reformation. If this failed to recover the lost principalities, it effectively erased any Protestant threat to the vast areas still under Catholic rule.

Population figures for the sixteenth century have a considerable margin of error, but the trends are fairly definite. Around the Mediterranean there was little change, in the North Sea–Atlantic area there was an increase of about 25 per cent and in Poland–Russia an increase of about 40 per cent during the century. The rapid increase in Eastern Europe was due to the continuing decline of the nomad, who was no longer able to cull the peasants or even to stop them edging onto his pasture.

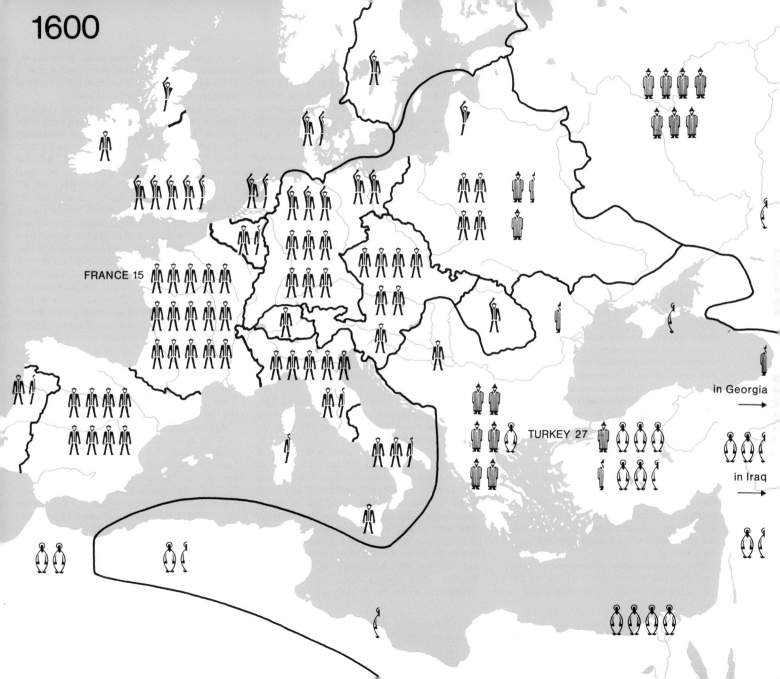

1600

FRANCE 15

TURKEY 27

in Georgia →

in Iraq →

Europe in 1600
3. Towns, Trade and Revenues

Europe became steadily more prosperous during the sixteenth century. Partly this was due to intrinsic factors – population and productivity were both rising – partly it was a consequence of the expansion of the market following the voyages of discovery. However, contemporary opinion, which equated wealth with precious metals, put it all down to the influx of silver from Mexico and Peru. On this theory, not only should Spain have become richer, which in terms of government revenue it did, but the Spaniards should have become the most prosperous people in Europe. And this they certainly did not.

The New World colonists needed manufactures. Spain was a primary producer and not going to change into a commercial nation overnight – particularly as Spanish society, obsessed with a medieval concept of status, found it difficult to change at all. Still, it was not unreasonable to expect that what Spanish industry there was would benefit from colonial demand. Unfortunately, the deleterious consequences of the silver inflow more than cancelled out the advantages of a theoretically protected market. The mechanism was unappreciated but simple. Because more money could only find expression in higher prices, a ripple of price increases spread across Europe every time a new silver consignment arrived at Seville. The effect being felt first and most fiercely in Spain, the country permanently occupied top place in the inflationary table. Spanish costs became increasingly uncompetitive, Spanish industry steadily declined. However protectionist the policy, the cheaper goods of the North Europeans – the Netherlanders in particular – could not be kept out of Spain, or out of the holds of the Spanish ships that sailed to the Americas.

The 'price revolution' of the sixteenth century – caused not only by the imports of silver but also by the increasing velocity of circulation that went with a more vigorous commercial life – was accompanied by a rise in wages. However, this was only about half as fast as the rise in prices, so the real value of wages declined. The result was a redistribution of wealth in favour of the entrepreneurs. Once again it was the Netherlands, at the centre of the North European commercial network, that reaped the harvest.

These underlying economic trends in favour of the Netherlands explain the ability of the Dutch to sustain the long struggle for independence. The division that the revolt imposed on the country was followed by a shift in its economic centre to the free North: conservative Belgium barely held its old level (Antwerp actually declined), while revolutionary Holland boomed and Amsterdam became the fastest-growing city in Europe. In Amsterdam the merchant evolved into the capitalist, conscious of costs as well as profits, of turnover as well as mark-up. The efficiency of this new society is apparent in its most essential aspect – shipping. Both the initial price and the operating costs of Dutch ships were a good third below anyone else's. By the end of the sixteenth century the Dutch alone were as strong as the whole Netherlands had been at the beginning and Dutch growth was still accelerating.

While the North prospered Italy stagnated. Venice is the paradigm and the Portuguese discovery of the Cape route to the East is at first sight the obvious explanation. But, in fact, the volume of spices brought to Europe doubled in the course of the sixteenth century and half the traffic stuck to the traditional ways that ended up at Venice. There was some fall in prices and profitability as a result of the increase in volume, some disruptions (as always) due to Ottoman bellicosity, but neither of these were critical. What really put Italy and the Mediterranean in second place behind the Dutch and the North Sea was the higher cost of its goods and services. By the middle of the century Venetian ships had stopped sailing to the Netherlands: by its end English and Dutch ships were entering the Mediterranean in increasing numbers. Moreover, though the Venetian fleet in 1600 was still as big as it had been in 1500, half of its larger ships were now Dutch-built.

The commodities of trade remained much the same during the sixteenth century but some of the sources changed. Mediterranean sugar was already being undercut by new plantations in the Canaries when Columbus discovered America: Brazilian sugar was soon undercutting both. The only other major New World export (apart from the all-important silver) was leather, first from the Antilles, then from Mexico. Inside Europe the significant changes are in scale. Statistics at this date are dodgy but annual coal production jumped from about 300,000 tons in 1500 (Belgian and British in a 2 : 1 ratio) to about 1,000,000 tons in 1600 (in a 3 : 7 ratio). Less dramatic but eloquent of increasing concern with costs are the figures for Swedish iron exports. These rose from a bare 1,000 tons in 1500 (which would be less than 1 per cent of a total production of about 125,000 tons for the area covered by the map) to 5,000 tons in 1600 (over 3 per cent of a total of perhaps 150,000 tons). Europe was becoming one market: whereas in 1500 wheat prices varied from low-cost Baltic to high-cost Mediterranean producers by a factor of seven, by 1600 the factor was down to five.

Approximate government revenues for the year 1600 are as follows (figures in millions of Venetian ducats): Castile 7·8 plus 2 in American silver; France 5·5; Ottoman Empire 4; Naples 3; Venice, Portugal 2; Milan 1·5; Dutch Republic 1·1; England 0·9; Aragon, Sicily 0·6; Austria, Savoy, Poland 0·5. The cumulative total for the Spanish Empire (15·5) somewhat overstates its resources because of the faster rate of inflation in Spain and her possessions vis-à-vis the rest of Europe.

In 1600 the urban population of Europe reached 5 per cent of the total, as against 2½ per cent at the beginning of the century. In the Netherlands the proportion reached 15 per cent.

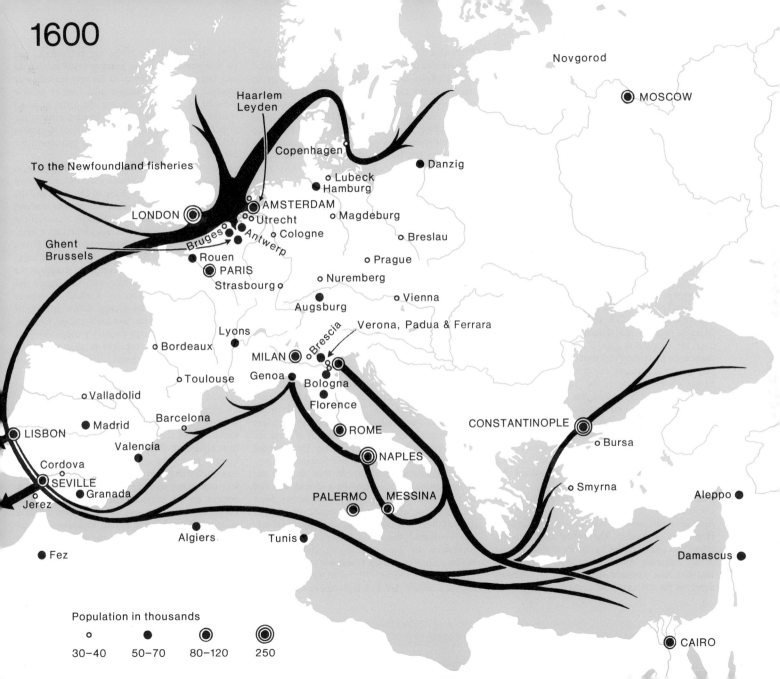

1600

Novgorod

MOSCOW

To the Newfoundland fisheries

Haarlem
Leyden

Copenhagen

Danzig

Lubeck
Hamburg

LONDON

AMSTERDAM

Utrecht

Magdeburg

Bruges

Antwerp

Cologne

Breslau

Ghent
Brussels

Rouen

PARIS

Strasbourg

Prague

Nuremberg

Vienna

Augsburg

Verona, Padua & Ferrara

Lyons

Brescia

Bordeaux

MILAN

Toulouse

Genoa

Bologna

Valladolid

Florence

Barcelona

CONSTANTINOPLE

LISBON

Madrid

ROME

Bursa

Valencia

NAPLES

Cordova

SEVILLE

Granada

PALERMO

MESSINA

Smyrna

Aleppo

Jerez

Algiers

Tunis

Damascus

Fez

Population in thousands

o
30–40

●
50–70

◉
80–120

◎
250

CAIRO

Europe in 1634
Political Units

By turning Catholic and at the same time promising toleration for Protestants, Henry IV of France re-unified his country. His minister Sully revived its finances and an easy war with Savoy brought valuable additions round Lyons in compensation for the loss of Saluzzo (1601). By 1610 Henry was all set for another try at breaking out of the Spanish ring. His assassination that year put an end to his programme and to strong government in France. The first decade of Louis XIII's reign was disfigured by the quarrels of aristocratic cliques and it was only with the advent to power of Cardinal Richelieu in 1624 that France once again became capable of an active foreign policy.

At the other end of Europe Russia passed into a disastrous 'time of troubles' on the death of Boris Godunov in 1605. Godunov had ruled on behalf of Ivan the Terrible's idiot son Feodor, then, after Feodor's death in 1598, in his own name. But he failed to found a new dynasty and the confusion over the succession gave Russia's enemies their chance. In 1611 the Poles took Smolensk, in 1612 they occupied Moscow and put the Polish Crown Prince on the throne of the Tsars. In 1613 the Swedes occupied Novgorod. But this was the turning point: the same year a national uprising ejected the Poles from the capital and the Russians got a native Tsar again – Michael Romanov, son of the Patriarch of Moscow. At the cost of considerable cessions of territory peace was made with Sweden (1617) and Poland (1618). Russia licked her wounds and waited.

The centre of European tension moved to Germany. In 1618 the Protestants of Bohemia rose in revolt against the rule of the Catholic Hapsburgs of Austria. The Bohemian crown was offered to and accepted by the Protestant Elector of the Palatinate. Such blatant indifference to the legalities that obsessed the Princes of Germany deprived the Elector of all support: no important

Protestant backed him and though Ferdinand II of Austria was too weak to attack anyone he enlisted both Catholic Bavaria and Protestant Saxony in the Hapsburg cause. The Bavarian general Tilly conquered Bohemia and the Upper Palatinate, the Saxons Lusatia and Silesia (1620). Then with Spanish help Tilly conquered the Rhine Palatinate (1622). Ferdinand rewarded his allies generously: the Saxons got Lusatia, the Bavarians the Upper Palatinate (and the Palatinate's electoral vote) while the Spanish got Upper Alsace. His own resources were greatly increased. If he had acquired Bohemia by peaceful inheritance his power there would have suffered the traditional restrictions: the massive confiscations of territory that followed the repression of the rebellion gave him an effective grip on the nation and its wealth.

In 1623 Tilly moved into North Germany and scattered the small Protestant forces still under arms. The Danes – who had claims on various border areas – attempted to exploit Protestant fear of Tilly's Catholic army and took Lower Saxony under their protection. This protection was illusory as Tilly proved by an easy victory at Lutter (1626). Backing Tilly up in this campaign was a second army which obeyed Ferdinand's orders. Raised and led by Albrecht von Wallenstein, Ferdinand's proconsul in Bohemia, this force made possible a specifically Hapsburg policy. When Ferdinand ordered Wallenstein to clear Mecklenburg, Germany became aware of plans for a Hapsburg dominion on the Baltic. This alarmed the Swedes, who put troops into Stralsund to prevent Wallenstein taking it. It also alarmed the German princes who – regardless of religion – had no wish to see an Emperor with real power. Now the Bohemian affair had been settled, the princes insisted, there was nothing more to fight about: unless Ferdinand wanted to hazard the Hapsburg succession to the Empire he must dismiss Wallenstein. Reluctantly Ferdinand agreed.

By this time Cardinal Richelieu was in charge of France's affairs. He had high hopes of profiting

from the continuation of the war in Germany and no intention of allowing peace to break out just to suit German convenience. At the very least the war engaged Hapsburg energies and, just as he was subsidizing the Dutch against the Spanish, so he would do the same for the Swedes against the Austrian Hapsburgs. In Sweden's King Gustavus Adolphus he perceived the perfect instrument for his policy.

Gustavus had come to the throne of Sweden in 1611, when he was seventeen years old. His crown was claimed by both the King of Denmark and the King of Poland; his kingdom was so poor that one wonders why they bothered. Besides war with the Danes and Poles Gustavus also inherited a long-standing conflict with Russia over Finland. Given that such armies as Sweden could raise were regularly defeated by everyone except the Russians, the obvious move was to settle with the Danes and Poles and concentrate on Finland. Gustavus managed to buy off the Danes with a promise of 400,000 ducats (twice Sweden's annual revenue, but rising prices for the country's copper exports enabled him to clear the debt in four years): the Poles agreed to a truce because they too were eager to exploit the 'time of troubles' in Russia. Gustavus made good use of the opportunity he had created: the treaty he eventually extracted from Moscow gave him not only the disputed borderlands of Finland but the province of Ingria on the south side of the Gulf as well (1617). Gustavus then turned on Poland. A series of campaigns in Livonia tested the new equipment and tactics he was introducing into the army:[1] by 1626 Livonia was conquered and the army battle-hardened. A descent on the Prussian coast demonstrated that Gustavus was now master of the Eastern Baltic: a reluctant Poland finally agreed to a new truce on the basis of the existing situation. This included Swedish garrisons in all the Prussian ports: the tolls they extracted doubled Gustavus's revenue and paid for his more than doubled forces.

Richelieu's envoys had arranged this truce: they

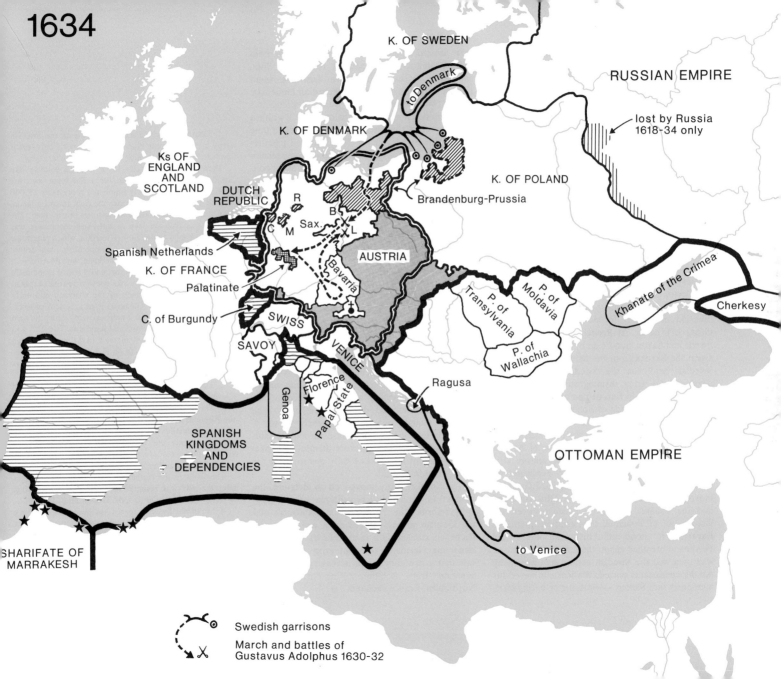

1634

K. OF SWEDEN

RUSSIAN EMPIRE

to Denmark

lost by Russia
1618-34 only

K. OF DENMARK

Ks OF
ENGLAND
AND
SCOTLAND

DUTCH
REPUBLIC

K. OF POLAND

Brandenburg-Prussia

R

B

C

Sax.

M

L

AUSTRIA

Spanish Netherlands

K. OF FRANCE

Bavaria

Palatinate

P. of
Transylvania

P. of
Moldavia

Khanate of the Crimea

Cherkesy

C. of Burgundy

SWISS

SAVOY

VENICE

P. of
Wallachia

Ragusa

Genoa

Florence

Papal State

OTTOMAN EMPIRE

SPANISH
KINGDOMS
AND
DEPENDENCIES

SHARIFATE OF
MARRAKESH

to Venice

Swedish garrisons

March and battles of
Gustavus Adolphus 1630-32

next offered Gustavus an annual subsidy of 200,000 ducats if he would invade Germany. Gustavus needed no prompting: he had watched with dismay the advance of the Hapsburg powers and was eager to take offensive action to protect both his co-religionists and his Baltic hegemony. In 1630 he landed in Pomerania with 20,000 men.

The German princes – even the Protestant ones – were not pleased to see him. The Elector of Brandenburg had cause to be sore, for in 1618 he had inherited the Duchy of Prussia (under Polish suzerainty) and most of the port dues that Poland had just surrendered to Sweden really belonged to him.[2] The Elector of Saxony was in no mood to dispute with the Hapsburgs for even if the Protestants elsewhere in Germany had suffered, Saxony had gained Lusatia. Both made it clear that there was no question of an anti-Catholic crusade. Gustavus took no notice. In early 1631 he bullied the Elector of Brandenburg into a definite alliance: in September the same year Tilly's unprovoked invasion of Saxony forced its Elector too into Gustavus's camp. At Breitenfeld (B on the map) Swede and Saxon stood side by side. Tilly's attack swept the Saxons from the field but broke on the Swedish flank: as the Swedish counter-attack developed his army disintegrated. Overnight the balance of power in Europe had changed.

Leaving the invasion of Bohemia to the Saxons, Gustavus marched westward to the Rhine. He spent the winter of 1631/2 in the Palatinate raising huge German armies for an invasion of Bavaria and Austria in the next campaigning season. Tilly fell back on Bavaria: a desperate Ferdinand recalled Wallenstein. In the spring of 1632 Gustavus moved against Bavaria, knocked Tilly aside and laid the country waste. Wallenstein forced the Saxons out of Bohemia, then cautiously entered Bavaria. He stood off Gustavus's attack and Ferdinand breathed again: the campaigning season was over and the Swedish assault had been held. As the combatants parted, Wallenstein moved his men north into Saxony – wintering on enemy terri-

tory seemed a shrewd move in terms of both politics and supply. Gustavus raced after him, caught his forces as they were dispersing round Lutzen (L on the map) and launched an immediate assault. He was a shade too quick. Wallenstein's second-in-command, Pappenheim, was still within a day's march of the battlefield and got back in time to take the Swedes in the flank. Locked together the armies fought themselves out. Pappenheim was mortally wounded in the early afternoon: Gustavus, leading a cavalry charge, took a musket-ball in the arm, was swept into the mêlée, unhorsed by a bullet in the back and shot dead as he lay. The Swedes wavered, rallied, attacked again. By nightfall they held the battlefield and Wallenstein was in retreat.

After Lutzen the legendary days of the Swedish expeditionary force were over, but offensive power still lay in the Swedish rather than the Imperialist camp. Particularly as Wallenstein seemed about to strike out on his own account and Ferdinand had to have him murdered. Then in 1634 Madrid agreed that a new Spanish army, which was due to pass from Italy via Germany to the never-ending war in the Low Countries, could co-operate with the Imperialist army during its passage.[3] Near the little Bavarian town of Nordlingen the united forces of the Hapsburg world came face to face with the Swedes and their German allies. The Swedes, though outnumbered nearly 2 to 1, attacked: the Spanish held fast through assault after assault until the attackers themselves broke. The Protestant army was totally destroyed in the pursuit that followed.[4]

The Spanish army moved on to Belgium, the remnant of the Swedish expeditionary force gradually reformed in the north, the Hapsburgs and the German princes agreed to a general peace. Richelieu, still subsidizing the Swedes and the only remaining German Protestant army (in Alsace), saw that a new factor was necessary to keep the equation from solution. Nine months after Nordlingen, France declared war.

1. Mostly this was a matter of bringing the Swedish army up to European standards: Gustavus's only major innovation was the creation of a mobile field artillery.

There was no difficulty about a small country like Sweden raising enough men for a European war, for armies at this time rarely numbered more than 25,000 and all states had on the books the right to call a feudal levy which would produce many times this number. The trouble was that the levy of untrained manpower was totally useless in contemporary warfare, which required a professional level of skill and co-operation from arquebusier and pikeman. The fact that Spain, with its American silver, was the only country that could afford to maintain professional armies of any size goes far towards explaining the Spanish supremacy of the sixteenth and early seventeenth centuries. Gustavus used a system of selective conscription to raise a national army which he then trained and paid to professional standards. The trick was paying it. Despite a steady increase in the number of men under arms, he was able to do this because he was consistently successful and his conquests kept his coffers full.

2. The Elector of Brandenburg had also inherited Cleves, Mark and Ravensburg (C, M and R on the map).

3. The Spanish had always been prepared to act along the Rhine to keep their lifeline with Belgium open. They did occasionally attempt the sea passage to the Netherlands still: they lost a fleet off Zeeland in 1631 and a bigger one, a real armada, was destroyed by the Dutch admiral Tromp in English territorial waters in 1639.

The front in the Netherlands registered few changes after the war was resumed in 1620: the Spanish took Breda in 1625, the Dutch took Maastricht in 1632.

4. Important Swedish forces had been detached for a war against Poland. The Russians were attempting the recapture of Smolensk and the Swedes hoped for easy pickings. In the event the Poles held the Russians without much difficulty and, after Nordlingen, were able to force the Swedes to return the Polish ports they had held since 1629. Altogether it was a disastrous diversion for the Swedes.

For a year after Nordlingen it looked as though Ferdinand II was going to make the German Empire a real state and himself the first effective Emperor since medieval times. Bavaria (now occupying both halves of the Palatinate), Saxony (offered Magdeburg in addition to Lusatia) and Brandenburg (promised Pomerania, though it was still full of Swedes) agreed to Ferdinand's plans to strengthen his authority if their acquisitions were confirmed. But getting the German princes to agree was only half the battle: Ferdinand also had to prevent the French and Swedes from disrupting the settlement. No matter how high the price he should have bought off one or the other, but in the optimistic afterglow of Nordlingen he missed his chance. The Swedes re-grouped in the north-east, beat the Saxon and Imperial forces sent against them in 1636 and beat them again in 1638: by the end of that year they were raiding into Bohemia once more. The French-subsidized army in Alsace also went over to the offensive in 1638, crossing the Rhine to take Upper Baden. Ferdinand III (who had succeeded his father in 1637) found the structure he had taken over shakier than he had supposed.

The troubles that hit the Spanish Empire at the same time were even less expected. In 1640 attempts to get Aragon to pay taxes on the Castilian scale provoked Barcelona to flaming revolt. The rebels invited the French to resume the suzerainty of the county (which they had held in medieval times) and contribute to its defence: Richelieu was delighted to do so. Later the same year the Portuguese also raised the standard of rebellion. Their overseas empire had not prospered since the union with Spain and they wanted a king of their own again. Spanish attempts to crush these revolts failed miserably: instead of sending reinforcements to the battlefields of Europe, Madrid was calling on Brussels and Milan for aid.

43

Leaving the impossible logistics aside, Brussels could spare nothing. What had been an offensive war against the Dutch had become a holding operation against Dutch and French and though the army in the Netherlands was Spain's best it was hard put to it to maintain a two-way defence. In 1637 the Dutch recaptured Breda. In 1643 came the French challenge. The Duc d'Enghien, hand-picked by Richelieu to command the French army in its first major offensive, moved against a marginally stronger Spanish force besieging the frontier fortress of Rocroi. Taking command of the cavalry of the French right, Enghien defeated his opposite number, struck across the centre of the field and hit the flank of the Spanish right-wing cavalry just as the French left was beginning to break. The Spanish horse scattered, leaving the foot to face the whole French army. Spanish cavalry had no exceptional reputation: the *tercios*, the regiments of professional infantry that had upheld the Spanish hegemony for over a century, were a different matter. It took a long afternoon of artillery fire and combined cavalry and infantry assaults to break them. Once the job was done, there was no quarter. Rocroi was not just a Spanish defeat: it was the destruction of an irreplaceable instrument.

Things went no better for the Austrian Hapsburgs. At the second battle of Breitenfeld in 1642 the Swedes crushed the Imperial forces as completely as they had at the first. The Swedes then took 1643 off to beat up the Danes, but the respite brought little comfort to Ferdinand III, who had the news of Rocroi to digest. His reaction was swift and sensible: a peace conference was opened in Westphalia at which Ferdinand made no secret of the fact that he was dropping the whole Imperial idea. Eventually, after four years of negotiation, the conflicting claims of the various belligerents were reconciled and the treaty was signed.

There was no doubt who the victors were. Sweden got Western Pomerania, Wismar and Bremen–Verden plus a two million ducat indemnity. (She also got the islands of Bornholm and Oesel, a couple of Norwegian provinces and the west coast of Gothland as the result of her walkover war with Denmark.) France obtained outright possession of her Moselle bridgehead and of Upper Alsace plus a purposely ill-defined suzerainty over the rest of Alsace. These gains put the whole block of territory between the old French frontier and the Upper Rhine within the French grasp.

Inside Germany small-scale rearrangements reflected the end of the Imperial and Catholic ideal. The Rhine Palatinate and its electoral vote were restored to its original Protestant family. (Bavaria kept the Upper Palatinate and was given an electoral vote of its own.) Brandenburg got Halberstadt, Minden and the promise of Magdeburg to compensate for its losses in Pomerania. Saxony kept Lusatia. Ferdinand, who had managed to hold the Franco-Alsatian invasion of Bavaria and the Swedish invasion of Bohemia until the Treaty of Westphalia was safely signed, now breathed again. Apart from Lusatia and Upper Alsace — both signed away by his father — he had succeeded in keeping his hereditary dominions intact.

So ended the Thirty Years War, though not the Franco-Spanish conflict, which went on as before. A few months before the signing of the Treaty of Westphalia Enghien trapped and annihilated a second Spanish army at the battle of Lens, a defeat that more than counter-balanced the fact that the Dutch had just signed a definitive peace with Spain (the far-sighted Dutch were now more worried about French imperialism than Spanish).

While these events occupied the continent the English made their own history. King Charles I and his Parliament reached the parting of the ways in 1642 and in the civil war that followed the King was defeated, captured and imprisoned (1645). Three years later he succeeded in getting the Scots to take up his cause, but they were easily beaten by Parliament's general Cromwell. This second war only served to destroy the compromise Parliament still believed possible. When the victorious soldiers arrived back in London they brushed Parliament aside and put King Charles on trial for his life (1648). He was beheaded in the New Year, leaving a faithful Ireland to his son (and Scotland inclining the same way) but England a Commonwealth ruled by a military junta in which Cromwell was the dominant figure.

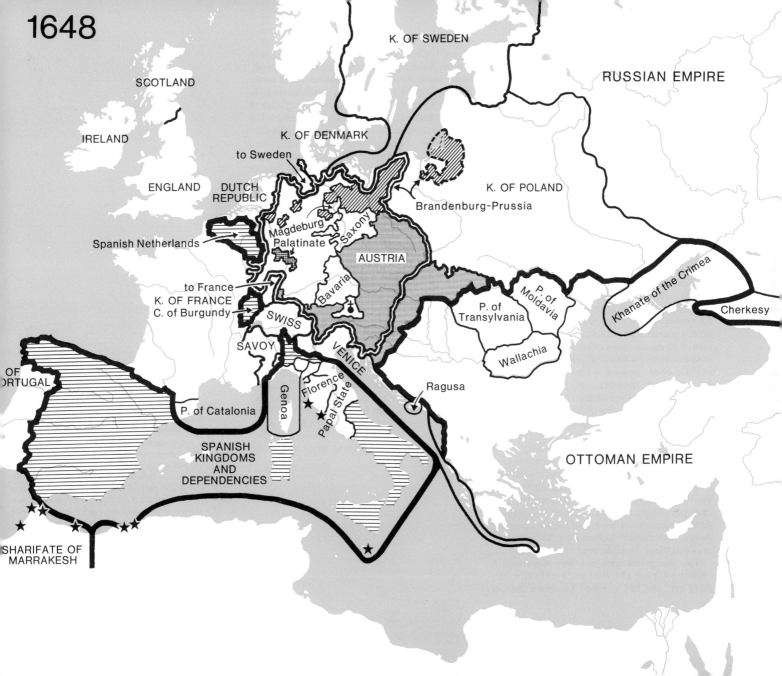

1648

SCOTLAND

IRELAND

K. OF SWEDEN

RUSSIAN EMPIRE

ENGLAND

K. OF DENMARK

to Sweden

DUTCH
REPUBLIC

K. OF POLAND

Brandenburg-Prussia

Spanish Netherlands

Magdeburg
Palatinate

Saxony

AUSTRIA

to France
K. OF FRANCE
C. of Burgundy

Bavaria

SWISS

SAVOY

VENICE

P. of
Transylvania

P. of
Moldavia

Wallachia

Khanate of the Crimea

Cherkesy

OF
PORTUGAL

P. of Catalonia

Genoa

Florence

Papal State

Ragusa

OTTOMAN EMPIRE

SPANISH
KINGDOMS
AND
DEPENDENCIES

SHARIFATE OF
MARRAKESH

The World in 1648
1. Population

The behaviour of the Spaniards in the New World was ruthless: recalcitrant natives were massacred; the submissive were enslaved. Driven to work on their new owners' properties and mines these unfortunates died by the thousand. The Caribbeans, who had originally numbered something over 100,000, were wiped out; in many mainland areas the population fell to a third of the pre-Columban level. At the low point, around 1600, there were probably only half as many people in the Americas as there had been a century before.

The ruthlessness of the *conquistadors* was perhaps exceptional even by sixteenth-century standards. The 'no quarter' tradition of the Crusader was very much alive in Spain (Granada fell only in 1492) and the conquest was a crusade among the godless. Fear of native numbers also encouraged the use of terror. But if Spaniards were harsh men, they compared favourably with the murderous Aztecs: tyranny was no new phenomenon in Mexico. In truth, the magnitude of the demographic catastrophe exonerates the *conquistadors*: no sixteenth-century people could contrive events on such a scale. The killers were European, but microbes, not men, and of the microbes, smallpox was the most important.

From the point of view of the smallpox virus the New World population was an ideal pabulum, being unselected genetically, naïve immunologically and, in Mexico, overcrowded. Mortality was exceptionally high from the start, and, as the virulence of a disease is increased by rapid spread, soon became higher. It was only after several generations that the Amerindians began to acquire resistance and their populations recover. In the mid seventeenth century numbers still fell short of the pre-Columban level, even counting in the immigrant (European) and imported (Negro) populations.[1]

The immigrants were not very numerous. A century and a half after the New World's discovery there were only half a million Europeans there, of whom 100,000 had settled in Brazil, 250,000 in Spanish America and 100,000 (half of them English) in the Lesser Antilles. The English colonies on the Atlantic coast of North America contained the additional 50,000 (the French of Canada and Dutch of New Netherland numbered a bare 1,000 each). The Negro total was under half the European and heavily concentrated in Brazil – plantation-style agriculture was as yet limited to the Brazilian speciality of sugar production. As the English colonies in the Antilles also began to produce sugar so their slave population rose rapidly (from 10 to 50 per cent in the decades on either side of 1648; the poorer English smallholders emigrated to North America leaving the total population much the same). These figures are all approximate: not only is information scanty but in Brazil and Spanish America the distinctions between European, Negro and Amerindian were already blurred by the presence of mulatto (European–Negro) and mestizo (European–Amerindian) populations as large as the pure European.[2]

All these changes are of little importance to the world total for 1648. Since 1483 the agricultural communities had increased their already large populations by sizable percentages: something between 30 and 40 per cent in Europe (to reach 100 million), China (now 175 million) and Japan (now 20 million), while India's growth of under 20 per cent (to 130 million) is still enough to make the *increase* in its population comfortably more than the New World's total. The Near Eastern zone, the Islamic heartland, is the only Old World area to show little or no growth.

1. Similarly, the New World's riposte, syphilis, which is now a rather slow and chronic affair, was an acute infection when it swept across Europe in the 1490s.

2. The yearly shipment of slaves from Africa to the New World in the period 1550–1650 seems to have been around 10,000, which means that something like a million Negroes must have been exported from Africa by 1648. The major part of the difference between this figure and the suggested New World population of quarter of a million is accounted for, not by the mortality of the voyage (which was about 20 per cent), nor even by the unfavourable sex ratio (two males were landed for every female), but by the inadequate reproduction rate that goes with the condition of slavery. A considerable part of each year's import went to make up this deficit. Only after the nineteenth-century emancipations did the Negro population become self-sustaining.

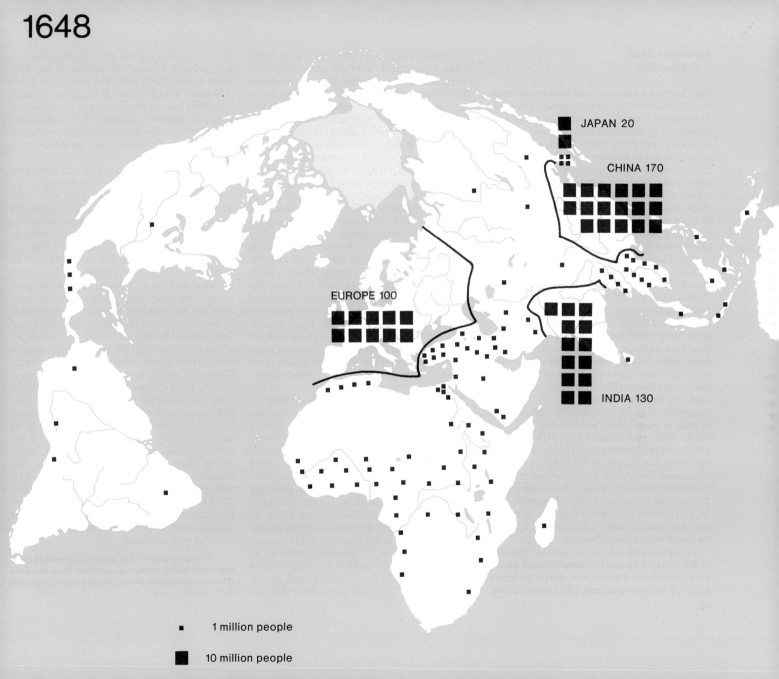

1648

JAPAN 20

CHINA 170

EUROPE 100

INDIA 130

■ 1 million people

■ 10 million people

The World in 1648
2. Political Units

The Dutch were somewhat slow to start their attack on the Spanish and Portuguese overseas empires, but when the attack came it was on a scale and in a mode appropriate to the world's leading maritime power. Where the English and French had confined themselves to raids and privateering, the Dutch moved in to stay, their aim being to destroy the Iberian trading network and replace it with one of their own. Profit lay in trade, not piracy, and though he had ample reason to hate Spain, the Dutchman loved a profit more than he hated anyone.

Portugal, at this time Spain's satellite, was the obvious first target for Dutch enterprise. In 1602 various Dutch companies which had established trading connections with Indonesia over the previous half dozen years were amalgamated to form the Vereenigde Ost-Indische Compagnie (Chartered East India Company), generally known as V.O.C. The progress of V.O.C. was triumphal, the Portuguese being driven out of the spice trade within a decade. In 1619 the V.O.C. man on the spot, Jan Coen, seized Jakarta from the Javanese and, under the name of Batavia, made it the capital of a V.O.C. empire that effectively monopolized the traffic in spices for the next two centuries. V.O.C. also replaced the Portuguese as the only Europeans allowed to trade in Japan (1641) and, working back westward, evicted the Portuguese from Malacca (1641) and Ceylon and Southern India (1638–58). Though the Portuguese clung on at isolated points such as Macao and Timor (and Spanish troops from the Philippines held the originally Portuguese fort on Tidore in the Moluccas till 1663) the commerce of the area between India, South-East Asia, Indonesia and Japan was now under V.O.C. control. It yielded the shareholders a steady dividend.

The success of V.O.C. encouraged the promotion of W.I.C. (the West India Company) to do a similar job in the Atlantic. Dutch investors were less happy about this and there was some difficulty in obtaining

an adequate subscription – the American terminals of the Atlantic trade were not isolated forts but proper colonies. On the other hand the Portuguese slaving stations in Africa were vulnerable and it might just be possible to conquer Brazil. W.I.C. (floated in 1621) got off to a good start with the seizure of Bahia, Brazil's capital (1624). However, the Portuguese recaptured it the next year and a further few years warfare, though successful in military terms, exhausted W.I.C.'s coffers. Admiral Piet Hein saved the day when he brought off the coup all privateers had dreamed of: capturing the Spanish Silver Fleet (1628). This enabled W.I.C. to pay a 75 per cent dividend and mount a second expedition against Brazil which seized Recife. Subsidiary expeditions established a fortified emporium on Curacao in the Caribbean (1634) and took the Portuguese slavers' ports in Guinea (El Mina, 1638) and West Africa (Luanda, 1641). But W.I.C. was still losing money and the Portuguese were still capable of the last effort needed to regain their most important Atlantic possessions: in 1648 they retook Luanda and in 1654 Recife. The W.I.C. attack had failed. It had not been fruitless however, for Dutchmen in one guise or another now had possession of most of the slave trade, and much of the general commerce of the Atlantic.

The period 1600–1648 saw the collapse of Spanish–Portuguese claims to legal ownership of the whole New World. The first successful colonies planted by non-Iberians were on the Atlantic coast of North America – Virginia (English, 1607), Acadia (French, 1605), New France (1608), Newfoundland (English, 1610), New England (1620) and New Netherland (1624). The Dutch also colonized Essequibo in Guyana in 1616. The next group was established in the Lesser Antilles – the first to be occupied were St Kitts and Barbados by the English in 1624 and 1627, and Guadeloupe and Martinique by the French in 1635. Within the Caribbean, as already mentioned, the Dutch took Curaçao in 1634 and in the Greater Antilles Frenchmen took possession of the islet of Tortuga off Hispaniola (1640). The

eonomy of these colonies was originally based on furs (in North America), privateering (in the Caribbean) or tobacco (in both). But whereas the North American colonies grew good-quality tobacco, Caribbean leaf was second-rate and the economy of the island settlements remained shaky until, around the date of this map, the plantation system of sugar-growing with slave labour was introduced from Brazil.

By 1648 the Cossack advance had carried the domain of the Tsars more than halfway across Siberia to Lake Baikal and the Lena river, while advance parties had reached the eastern edge of the continent. The most remarkable expeditions were those of Deshnev and Poyarkov. Deshnev sailed the final stretch of the northern coast, rounded the cape that now bears his name and passed through the Bering Strait (1647–8): his report was filed away in the local archives at Yakutsk, so Moscow never heard of his discoveries, but the voyage convinced Siberians that there was no land route to America. Poyarkov, travelling south-east from the Upper Lena, reached the Amur and sailed down it to the Sea of Okhotsk (1643–6).[1] He had a hostile reception when he tried to land on the right bank of the Amur, for the river was the northern frontier of the Chinese Empire. If the Chinese had still been ruled by the Ming this would not have been a matter of great importance, for Ming concern did not really extend beyond the southern half of Manchuria. But in the early seventeenth century the Ming Empire had disintegrated and the united Manchu tribes, in successful revolt against the Ming since 1626, had established their own dynasty in Peking in 1644. (A Ming prince still held the south-western provinces in 1648 but his days were numbered.) The Manchu Emperors were to pursue an aggressive frontier policy in which the perimeter of their original homeland was never neglected.

1. The Sea of Okhotsk had already been reached by an expedition taking a more direct route from the Lena (Moscovitin, 1639): a Dutch ship had a look round it a few years later.

1648

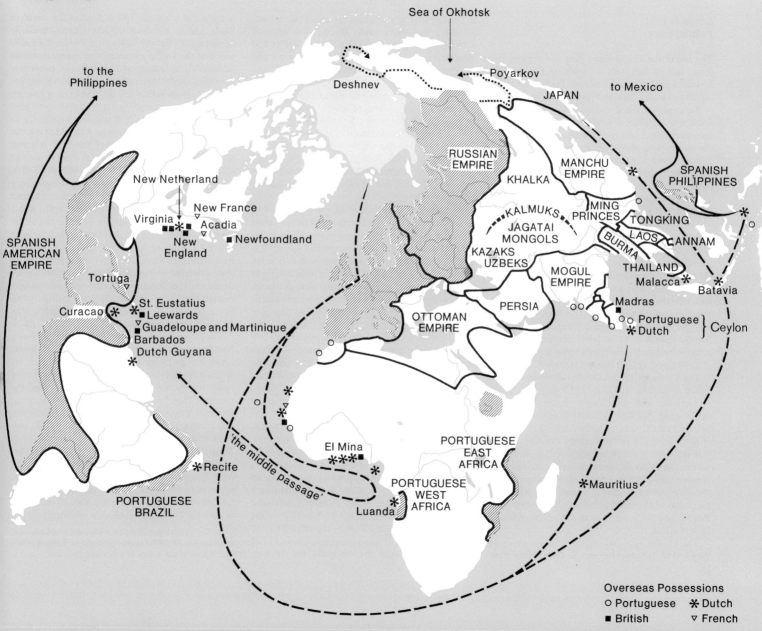

to the Philippines

Sea of Okhotsk

to Mexico

Deshnev

Poyarkov

JAPAN

RUSSIAN EMPIRE

MANCHU EMPIRE

KHALKA

SPANISH PHILIPPINES

New Netherland

New France

Virginia

Acadia

New England

Newfoundland

KALMUKS

MING PRINCES

TONGKING

JAGATAI MONGOLS

LAOS

BURMA

ANNAM

SPANISH AMERICAN EMPIRE

KAZAKS UZBEKS

THAILAND

Malacca

MOGUL EMPIRE

Batavia

Tortuga

PERSIA

Madras

Curacao

St. Eustatius

Leewards

Portuguese

Ceylon

Guadeloupe and Martinique

Dutch

Barbados

OTTOMAN EMPIRE

Dutch Guyana

'the middle passage'

El Mina

PORTUGUESE EAST AFRICA

Recife

PORTUGUESE WEST AFRICA

Luanda

Mauritius

PORTUGUESE BRAZIL

Overseas Possessions

○ Portuguese   ✳ Dutch

■ British   ▽ French

Europe in 1681
Political Units

The end of the Thirty Years War in Germany left Spain face to face with a victorious France. The Spanish Exchequer was bankrupt: the Spanish army was demoralized; the loss of Belgium and the County of Burgundy appeared imminent. But the final blow failed to materialize. The Parisian middle classes, fed up with high and arbitrary taxation, rebelled against the government of Richelieu's successor Mazarin. Enough French aristocrats disliked Mazarin on principle to give the movement the leadership it needed; Spain provided funds and arms. The year 1652 saw Enghien, the victor of Rocroi, leading a mercenary army to the occupation of Paris.

The rebel alliance was short-lived. The purely selfish aims of the aristocracy had no place in a programme of constitutional reform, and the middle classes soon decided that royal autocracy was preferable to feudal anarchy. By 1655 the rebellion (known as the Fronde after a hit-and-run children's game) was effectively over and both Mazarin and the situation on the war fronts had been restored. However, the Fronde had temporarily exhausted France and the French army certainly needed the English support arranged for its final campaigns. At the peace of 1659 Spain got off almost scot-free.[1]

The Cossacks of the Dnieper Bend repudiated Polish control in 1648: in 1653 they sought the protection of the Russian Tsar: in the consequent war the Russians had little difficulty in advancing their frontier to the Dnieper. The Polish King picked this of all moments to revive a purely dynastic quarrel with the Swedes, who, in company with the Brandenburgers, swept across the country and occupied both Warsaw and Cracow. Poland seemed about to disintegrate, but the Elector of Brandenburg withdrew his troops when promised full sovereignty over East Prussia, and the Swedes had to pull out because of a Danish attack.

The Swedes overwhelmed the Danes as easily as they had twelve years before (the Danish provinces in Sweden were now annexed for good) but this was Sweden's high-water mark. During fifty years of successful belligerence the list of her enemies had steadily lengthened. By themselves, the Danes and the Poles were too weak to be a threat, the Austrians too distant and the Russians as yet too ineffective. But the Dutch (who feared exclusion from a Swedish Baltic) and the Brandenburgers (who coveted Swedish Pomerania) were a different matter. In 1658 Dutch ships transported an army of Brandenburgers and others to the island of Fynen where the Swedes were badly defeated. Though France stepped in and prevented her old ally from being dispossessed of any of her territories, it was obviously time for Sweden to quieten down.

In 1659 Louis XIV came of age. The mood of France was in favour of autocracy and so was Louis. Thanks to the efficient finance minister, Colbert, the government's resources were steadily increasing: Louis immediately committed these resources to the glorification of himself, his court and his country – as far as he was concerned, the three were the same. Parisians being apt to express their own views on this theory, the court was moved to the nearby hamlet of Versailles. Building there continued throughout the reign, a work force that sometimes reached 30,000 men eventually producing a palace with a garden front nearly half a mile long. The pageant of monarchy appeared in a setting that was the envy of kings everywhere.

Abroad, Louis was faced with a political situation that could hardly have been better. France was rapidly recovering, Spain was not: the Dutch were ready to discuss a partition of Belgium. However, this was not Louis' way – no one was to share his glory – and in 1667–8 he invaded Belgium on his own account. The Dutch forced a truce with an ultimatum that had to be taken seriously because it was backed by England and Sweden. Louis soon broke up this 'triple alliance' by buying over the Swedes and the English. Then he launched his army down the Rhine and raced for Amsterdam (1672). The invasion looked overwhelming but, in fact, petered out when the Dutch flooded the country. Louis had to withdraw (he never campaigned in person again): the only lasting result of his onslaught was that the Dutch entrusted their government to William III of Orange and he dedicated himself to thwarting Louis. Moreover, the English, whose Protestant bias in favour of the Dutch was usually balanced by commercial enmity, began to be persuaded of the importance of stopping France. Louis could buy the king but not the people, and as it was a strictly limited monarchy that had been restored after Cromwell's death, the English Parliament was able to insist on a rapprochement with the Dutch (1674). The same year Austria and Brandenburg sent troops to fight on the Dutch side. Louis retaliated by setting Sweden on Brandenburg and on the whole had the better of the struggles in Belgium and on the Rhine. At the truce of 1678–9 he had to give Charleroi back to Spain but got the County of Burgundy, the recognition of a French protectorate over Lorraine and a bridgehead over the Upper Rhine. His diplomatic position was still strong enough for him to force Brandenburg to disgorge all but a fraction of its Pomeranian conquests (the Swedish attack there had misfired badly).

The Russo-Polish quarrel was settled in 1667 with Russia registering considerable gains – Smolensk, Chernigov and Kiev and a half-interest in the Cossacks of the Dnieper Bend (Kiev was supposed to be ransomed by the Poles but they never raised the money). The Turks also did well, thanks to an energetic dynasty of Grand Viziers, the Koprulu. The conquest of Crete was completed (1669), two more slices of Hungary were taken from Austria and Transylvania (1664, 1675), and Podolia together with the Polish half-interest in the Dnieper Cossacks from Poland (1672–6). But these successes were achieved against weak states which could not match the Ottoman capacity to sustain war: on the actual battlefields Turkish performance was mediocre.

1. The English got Dunkirk which the French bought off them for 700,000 ducats. Tangier, like Bombay, came to England as the dowry of a Portuguese queen.

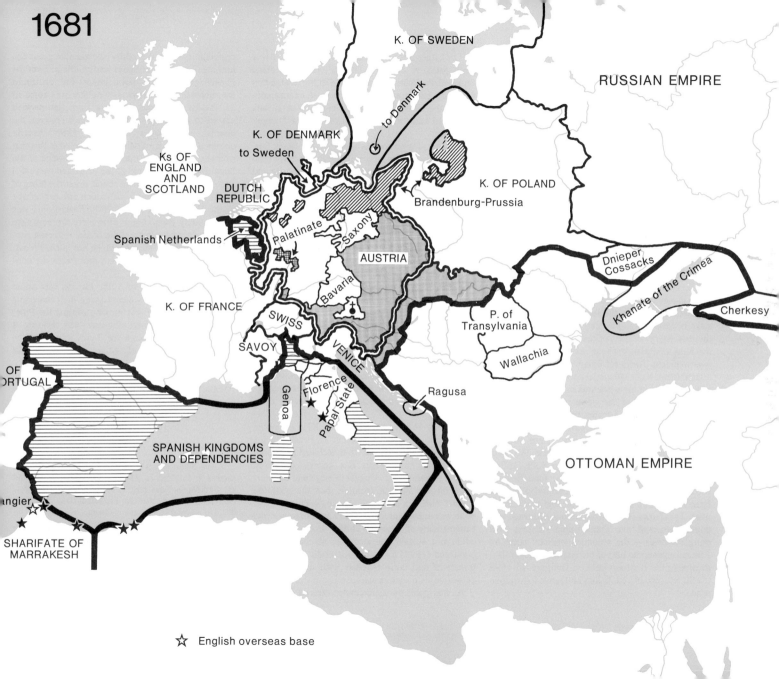

1681

K. OF SWEDEN

RUSSIAN EMPIRE

K. OF DENMARK

to Denmark

to Sweden

Ks OF ENGLAND AND SCOTLAND

DUTCH REPUBLIC

K. OF POLAND

Brandenburg-Prussia

Spanish Netherlands

Palatinate

Saxony

AUSTRIA

Bavaria

Dnieper Cossacks

Khanate of the Crimea

Cherkesy

K. OF FRANCE

SWISS

SAVOY

VENICE

P. of Transylvania

Wallachia

OF PORTUGAL

Genoa

Florence

Papal State

Ragusa

OTTOMAN EMPIRE

SPANISH KINGDOMS AND DEPENDENCIES

angier

SHARIFATE OF MARRAKESH

☆ English overseas base

Europe in 1701
Political Units

The key policy of the Koprulu Grand Viziers of Turkey was to keep the army busy: wars abroad meant peace at home. The long perimeter of the Empire could usually be relied on to provide at least one trouble spot: when all else failed old quarrels could be revived. In 1683 the best pretext available was the expiry of a twenty-year truce with the Austrians. Kara Mustapha, the third of the Koprulu viziers, decided to make a big thing of this. He personally led the army on what was to be its most spectacular foray for a century. The target was Vienna, the city that had withstood Suleiman the Magnificent and whose capture would be incontrovertible evidence of the success of Koprulu rule.

The Austrian capital was invested on schedule. After that everything went wrong. The Turkish artillery was inadequate, the defence vigorous and the siege bogged down. The Emperor had time to hire the mercenary services of the German princes and the King of Poland, whose relief army caught the overconfident Turks off balance and all but annihilated them. Kara Mustapha was garotted by order of the Sultan but his work was less easy to correct.

With the news of the victory a wave of excitement spread across Europe: the liberation of the Balkans appeared a real possibility. In an atmosphere redolent of the Crusades Venice and the Papacy pledged their support while Austrian armies moved down the Danube to Buda (1686), won a resounding victory on the fatal field of Mohacs (1687) and crossed the Danube to liberate Belgrade (1688). But that was the end of the walkover. The Turks reorganized, retook Belgrade and counter-attacked via Transylvania. It took two more victories – the second a brilliant coup by Prince Eugene, the best of the Hapsburg generals – to cement the Austrian hold on Hungary. In 1699 the Sultan recognized its loss and made a definitive peace.

The catastrope at Vienna allowed comparatively easy gains to Turkey's other enemies. Poland regained Podolia. Venice expanded her Dalmatian province and in a surprising burst of energy conquered the Pelóponnese. Tsar Peter of Russia took Azov and established full control over the Dnieper Cossacks.

Though pleased to gain a port in the Black Sea, Peter's real aim was a port on the Baltic. His ambition was to make Russia a western-style state and in a series of reforming decrees he savagely forced enlightenment on his cowering subjects. His genius was to realize that his reforms would die with him unless he placed Russia in geographical contact with the West. This contact could only be via the Baltic, which meant war with Sweden. Peter arranged an alliance with Denmark and Poland: all three declared war in 1700.

Sweden's King, the eighteen-year-old Charles XII, was a true descendant of Gustavus Adolphus. In August 1700 he knocked the Danes out of the war, in October he was on the opposite shore of the Baltic facing Peter's army in Estonia. In November the fury of his attack won the battle of Narva and sent the Russians reeling back in humiliation. He then went into winter quarters to ponder whether Poland or Russia should be his objective in the next campaign. His army was all of 10,000 strong.

Between 1689 and 1697 Louis XIV attempted to continue the aggrandizement of France in the face of a 'Grand Alliance' that included just about every power in Europe. His generals did well enough in an inching struggle of siege and counter-siege on the Belgian frontier, but the coalition against him stood firm – its Anglo-Dutch backbone was unbreakable once William of Orange had become King of England (1688).[1] In the end Louis could not sustain the struggle: at the Peace of Nymegen (1697) he had to surrender the few fortresses he had taken together with some of those gained in his previous wars.

At this point dynastic chance offered Louis the opportunity to make really spectacular gains for nothing. The King of Spain was childless: both the French and Austrian royal houses had claims to the succession. But obviously neither was going to get the lot. They and the other European powers agreed to a division by which France received the Spanish possessions in Italy while Austria obtained Belgium, Spain itself and the Spanish overseas Empire. No one took much notice of the Spanish (who were livid at the proposed carve-up) and it came as a complete shock when the King of Spain made a deathbed will which left everything to the French candidate (1700). Even Louis was momentarily nonplussed. However, the complete inheritance was something he could not resist and, though he knew it meant war, he accepted. French troops marched into Belgium and (with the connivance of Savoy) Milan.

So in the summer of 1701 Europe was under arms and the generals were issuing their marching orders. Charles XII was moving against the Poles on the Dvina. Prince Eugene was leading a Hapsburg army through the Tyrol to contest the French occupation of Milan. The Duke of Marlborough, William III's emissary on the continent, was marshalling the contigents of the Grand Alliance on the Lower Rhine.[2]

1. The Stuart (Scots) line of kings was never a great success in England. In 1688 James II's absolutist and pro-Catholic policies cost him his throne, which was offered by Parliament to his Protestant daughter Mary. She was married to William of Orange, who accepted on behalf of his wife and himself.

2. The Austrian Emperor had very little money but he could confer coveted titles. In 1692 Hanover had been raised to an electorate as a reward for its support of the Grand Alliance. In 1701 the Elector of Brandenburg was allowed to call himself 'King in Prussia' in return for his promise of help in the new war.

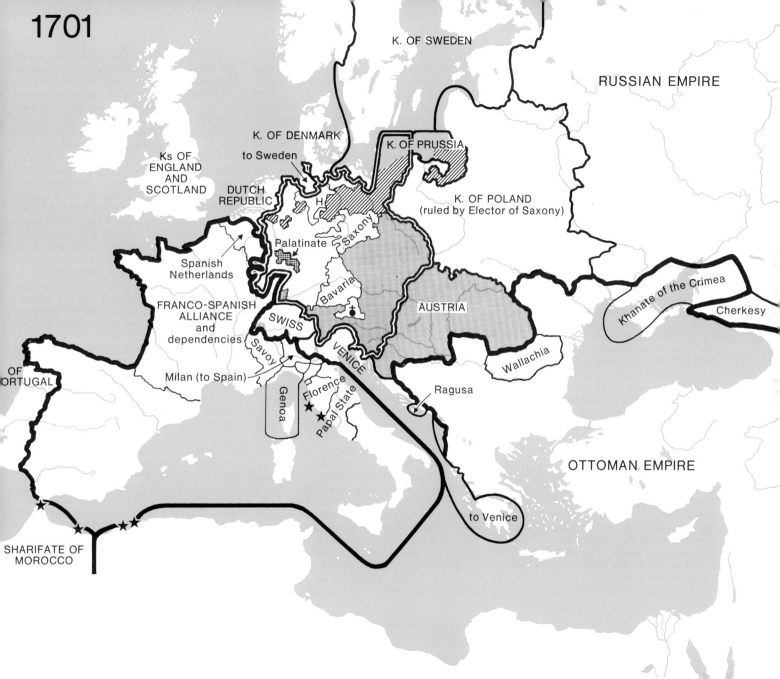

1701

K. OF SWEDEN

RUSSIAN EMPIRE

Ks OF
ENGLAND
AND
SCOTLAND

K. OF DENMARK
to Sweden

K. OF PRUSSIA

DUTCH
REPUBLIC

H.

Saxony

K. OF POLAND
(ruled by Elector of Saxony)

Palatinate

Spanish
Netherlands

Bavaria

AUSTRIA

FRANCO-SPANISH
ALLIANCE
and
dependencies

SWISS

VENICE

Khanate of the Crimea

Cherkesy

Savoy

Milan (to Spain)

Genoa

Florence

Papal State

Wallachia

Ragusa

OF
ORTUGAL

OTTOMAN EMPIRE

to Venice

SHARIFATE OF
MOROCCO

Europe in 1715
1. Political Units

In June 1701 Charles XII forced the Poles back from the Dvina. Since 1697 the Polish crown had been worn by Augustus, Elector of Saxony, and Saxon soldiers stiffened the Polish forces. Charles was so impressed by their fighting qualities that he decided to make his next campaign against Poland rather than Russia. In 1702 he took Warsaw, declared the Elector deposed from the Polish throne and installed a puppet king of his own. For the next three years he chased round Poland after Augustus: Tsar Peter in the interim doggedly moved back to the Baltic shore and – as an earnest of his total commitment to his programme – started to build his new capital, St Petersburg, on Swedish territory. In early 1706 Charles seemed to have got nowhere: to be precise he was in the east of Poland, having defeated yet another of the Russo-Polish armies that appeared each spring. However, that summer he solved his Polish problem by marching west, into Saxony. The occupation of his electorate brought Augustus to heel. He abdicated the Polish crown in favour of Charles's protégé, Stanislaus Leszczynski.

Charles was now free to tackle his real enemy, Peter of Russia. He set out in the summer of 1708, intending to be in Moscow by the autumn. The Russians in Eastern Poland fought better than expected. They also burnt the crops so thoroughly that Charles was out of supplies before he was over the frontier. If he couldn't go forward, he wouldn't go back: he turned south to the Ukraine. There his army was halved by the rigours of the Russian winter; in the spring the survivors were overwhelmed by Peter at the battle of Póltava (1709). All Sweden's enemies now closed in. By the time Charles got back home (via Turkey, 1715) nearly everything bar Sweden itself had been lost. He fought on till he was killed invading Norway (1718), then a series of treaties (1719–21) brought the 'Great Northern War' to an end. Sweden got

back Finland, Wismar and a sliver of Pomerania. The rest of Pomerania went to Prussia and Bremen–Verden to Hanover, while Peter got the Baltic provinces. St Petersburg was by then beginning to show the sparkle of a European capital: lugubrious Moscow was no longer the head of Russia, only the heart.

The Ottomans made a good recovery during this period. They defeated Peter and recovered Azov (1711); they drove the Venetians from the Peloponnese (1714). They did not have to fight the Austrians, who were fully committed against Louis XIV.[1]

The War of Spanish Succession (1701–13) was the last of Louis' wars. As his troops were in possession of the territories he hoped to acquire he began with a strong strategic advantage: tactically the French army had a fifteen-year record of victory behind it. Louis had every reason for confidence. William of Orange must have seen the war as a repeat of the previous struggle – an attritive process in which the superior resources of the Grand Alliance would eventually compel Louis to accept terms. William's death (1702) went a long way to negating this analysis. A general of dogged mediocrity who had insisted on heading the allied armies himself, his passing left the way clear for the Duke of Marlborough to take over the Anglo-Dutch forces.

The opening campaigns may have given Louis pause: both Marlborough in the Low Countries and Eugene in Italy outwitted the local French commanders. However, French losses were marginal and in the Bavarian Elector Louis found an ally to keep the Austrians busy. By 1704 a Franco-Bavarian army was threatening Vienna, forcing both Marlborough and Eugene to march to its defence. At Blenheim on the Upper Danube they brought the Franco-Bavarians to battle. From the first shot Marlborough and Eugene dominated the field. Ruthlessly pressed attacks on both flanks forced the French commander to weaken his centre; Marlborough's main force then split the

Franco-Bavarian army in two, pinned the southern half against the river and compelled its surrender. The spell of French invincibility was broken.

For the next few years everything went wrong for the French. Their worst year was 1706, when Marlborough won the battle of Ramillies and chased them out of the Spanish Netherlands, and Eugene won the battle of Turin and chased them out of Italy. Louis was back where he had started from and Marlborough and Eugene's final victories at Oudenard and Malplaquet (1708–9) made sure that he stayed there. The allies' attempt to conquer Spain failed, but as Louis was prepared to recognize that his grandson, now King of Spain, would be forever excluded from the French succession this should not have been a major obstacle to peace. In fact it was, and the war dragged on until the British[2] suddenly deserted their allies. At the treaty of Utrecht (1713), Austria got the ex-Spanish Netherlands, Milan, Naples and Sardinia. Savoy got Sicily. The British, who had deployed a fleet in the Mediterranean, kept the bases they had seized there.

As for Louis, he got his pre-war frontiers plus the prestige of having a member of his family on the throne of Spain. The price was high. Arrogance had isolated France diplomatically: defeat had tarnished her arms. The country was so exhausted and impoverished that it would take a generation to rebuild her political and military position. At the beginning of Louis' reign the eyes of Europe had been fixed on Versailles: fifty years later the Sun King still held court in the same superb style, but the world went its way. Well, that's show business.

1. Between 1701 and 1715 the Barbary States – Algiers, Tunis and Tripoli – passed out of Ottoman control. The Algerians took advantage of the war in Spain to seize Oran and Mers el-Kebir (1708): the Spanish took them back in 1732.

2. English and Scots became British with the Union of 1707. The crown was inherited by the Elector of Hanover in 1714 but this German connection was and remained purely dynastic.

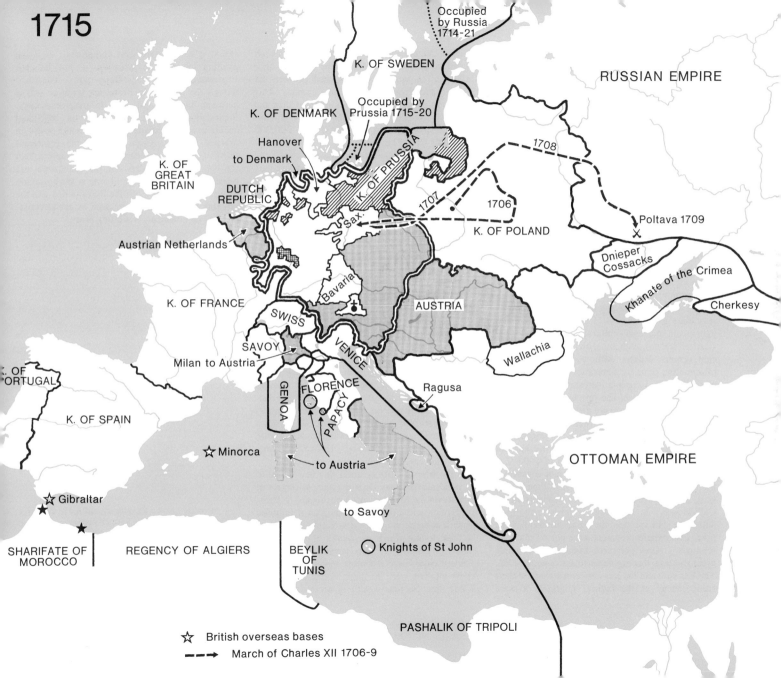

1715

Occupied
by Russia
1714-21

RUSSIAN EMPIRE

K. OF SWEDEN

K. OF DENMARK
Occupied by
Prussia 1715-20

Hanover
to Denmark

K. OF
GREAT
BRITAIN

DUTCH
REPUBLIC

K. OF PRUSSIA

1708

1707

1706

Poltava 1709

Austrian Netherlands

Sax.

K. OF POLAND

Dnieper
Cossacks

Khanate of the Crimea

Bavaria

AUSTRIA

Cherkesy

K. OF FRANCE

SWISS

SAVOY

Milan to Austria

VENICE

Wallachia

Ragusa

GENOA

FLORENCE

PAPACY

K. OF
PORTUGAL

K. OF SPAIN

☆ Minorca

to Austria

OTTOMAN EMPIRE

☆ Gibraltar
★

★

to Savoy

SHARIFATE OF
MOROCCO

REGENCY OF ALGIERS

BEYLIK
OF
TUNIS

◯ Knights of St John

PASHALIK OF TRIPOLI

☆ British overseas bases
▪▪▪➤ March of Charles XII 1706-9

Europe in 1715
2. Population and Religion

Each symbol represents 1 million people, Catholic, Protestant, Orthodox or Moslem

Between 1600 and 1715 the population of Europe increased from 90 to 118 million, a rise of 30 per cent. Top of the growth league, with an increase from 1 m. to 2·5 m., was Ireland. Irish multiplication was the beginning of a tragic Malthusian exercise: the recently introduced potato enabled the poverty-stricken peasantry to grow at a rate which prevented any escape from poverty. Whereas Scotland, with a moderate 33 per cent increase, entered the eighteenth century in good shape, the 'age of enlightenment' saw Ireland fall further and further behind the rest of northern Europe. The danger of dependence on a single crop is usually taken as the lesson of Ireland's population explosion, culminating as it did in the Great Famine of 1846–7: in fact the lasting damage to Irish society was done in the period of mounting population figures and increasing cultural deprivation.

After Ireland, with its growth rate of 150 per cent, comes Russia with about 75 per cent (discounting gains by annexation). This rate had a perfectly healthy basis in increasing peasant colonization of the steppe. The rest of Europe attained something near the average growth rate of 30 per cent except for mis-governed Spain and the exploited Balkans. Islam continued to stagnate.

In terms of blocs the religious demography of 1715 shows little change from that of 1600. The Orthodox area expanded, the Russian advance at the expense of Poland coming just in time to prevent the Orthodox there from conversion to Catholicism. A tendency towards uniformity within the state is indeed the significant trend of the time. Everywhere pressures were put on minority religious groups, pressures ranging from simple fiscal and legal disadvantages to active persecution. The less sure and the less concerned changed their habits, many of the faithful migrated or were expelled. As the minorities exchanged the Dutch became steadily more Calvinist, the Belgians more Catholic. The same thing happened between the Catholic and Protestant areas of Germany. This continuing process was more important than the dramatic expulsions – a quarter of a million Moslems from Spain in 1600–16, 200,000 Huguenots from France (1685).

Cataloguing these persecutions gives the impression that religion was playing as large a part in European life as ever. This is probably true of the first half of the seventeenth century, when increasingly effective state machinery was frequently employed in support of bigotry: it is certainly not true of the second half, by which time public sentiment – at least in northern Europe – was shifting in favour of tolerance. Religious feeling and religious institutions entered on a definite decline: from this time on the proportion of social behaviour influenced by religious beliefs diminished with each generation.

As the hold of the church slackened the men of science made their appearance. In 1600 their number was pathetically few, their thought hobbled by medieval preconceptions and their language contorted by the need to contain the hypotheses of antiquity. Throughout the century their number grew, the freedom to speculate increased, the language simplified and the new discipline of empirical trial gathered strength. The roll call of names is that of the founding fathers of the modern world: Galileo, Descartes, Harvey, Hooke, Newton, Boyle, Huygens, Malpighi, Leeuwenhoek.

In the course of its creation this new world of the mind moved away from the ancient centres of learning on the Mediterranean northward to Paris, Amsterdam and London. In doing so it followed the shift in the economic centre of gravity: this was the triangle into which the wealth of Europe was gathered. Here were the largest and fastest-growing cities, here the most demanding trades. Above all, here were the most literate populations of any size. Surplus wealth is necessary if education is to be more than exceptional; so is the printing press. The equation is not between Protestantism and scientific genius – cherished though the belief is in Protestant tradition – it is between literacy and the progressive society. Protestants with their emphasis on individual access to a vernacular Bible placed more stress on literacy than the Catholics, and the Protestant third of Europe was certainly more literate than the Catholic remainder. But the same area was probably richer and more literate at the beginning of the Reformation. Both the Reformation and the scientific revolution can be seen as social consequences of Gutenberg's printing press.[1]

1. Medieval literacy was almost confined to the clergy and merchants and cannot have exceeded 5 per cent of the adult male population. After the spread of printing the rate rose steadily to reach (by 1715) 50 per cent or more in the Protestant north, 25 per cent or less in the Catholic south. Some but by no means all of this difference relates to greater urbanization; townsmen always being more literate than country folk.

1715

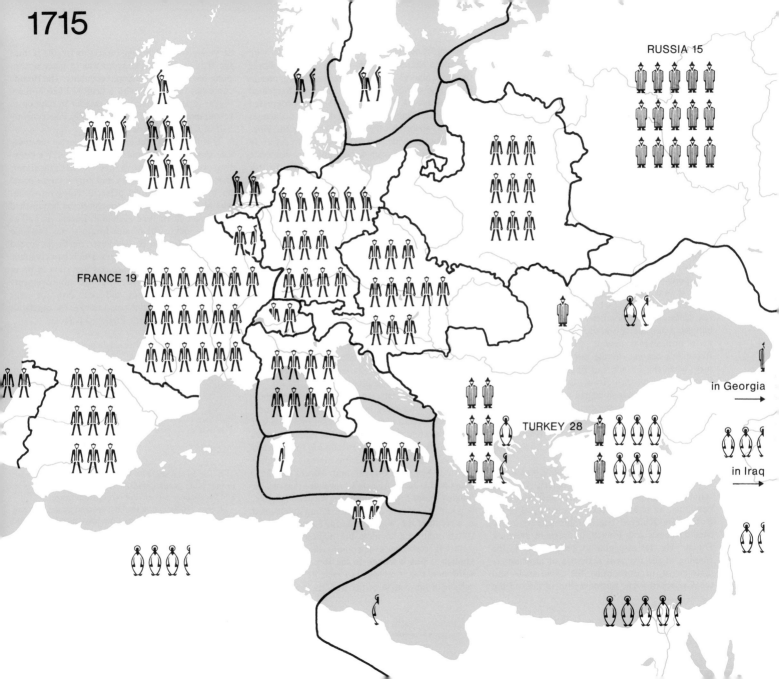

RUSSIA 15

FRANCE 19

TURKEY 28

in Georgia →

in Iraq →

In terms of trading volume and tonnage of shipping the Dutch lead over the rest of the world increased in the first half of the seventeenth century. The turning point came in the 1650s and 1660s where the English enacted a series of protectionist shipping laws and backed them up with an aggressive naval policy. In the resulting trio of Anglo-Dutch sea wars battle honours were evenly divided but the English made their point. The rapidly expanding trade of England which had previously benefited the Dutch as much as the English now became the exclusive preserve of English carriers: the tonnage of English-owned shipping began to rise steeply. In 1715 the Dutch merchant marine was till the bigger of the two but the crossover point was only twenty years away.

If it was English belligerence rather than English victories that forced the Dutch to share the sea lanes, the development of the purpose-built battleship and the appearance of the fighting navy as a professional service set the seal on the Republic's decline. In the later seventeenth century, when the French and English were building fleets of the new men-of-war, the Dutch dropped out of the race. Their ships had to earn their bread and if an East Indiaman could no longer take a place in the line of battle then the Royal Navy of their British ally (for we have now reached the period of the Grand Alliance against Louis XIV) would have to do the fighting for them.

France's attempt to pull off the same trick as the British was organized by Colbert. He discriminated against Dutch imports and built up a navy that, on paper at least, was the equal of the British. He achieved considerable success in the Mediterranean and French trade there overtook Dutch.[1] He was also able to keep France in the running in the overseas activities of most immediate profit to Europeans: the slave trade and the Caribbean sugar business. But in the end the preoccupation of his master Louis XIV with European aggrandizement ruined his plans. Louis treated Colbert's tariffs as a bargaining counter in negotiations with the Dutch, and soon bargained them away; as his continental wars progressed from sterile victory to ruinous defeat so his armies began to absorb all the men and money the kingdom could provide; the navy was left to rot away in port. Without having to fight any very desperate actions, indeed almost by default, the British became rulers of the high seas.

By 1715 England's rising prosperity had carried London to twice the size of Amsterdam. This metropolitan expansion increased the demand on industries that were to prove growth points elsewhere in the economy. English coal production (for which London was the main market) rose from 700,000 tons in 1600 to 3,000,000 in 1715 (about 85 per cent of total European production). To pump the water from the deeper mines Newcomen built the first steam engine, a version of which was operating on Tyneside by 1708. The next year the Midland ironmaster Abraham Darby began the first in a long-drawn-out series of attempts to smelt iron ore with coke. A process of this type was badly needed, for deforestation had reduced charcoal supplies to famine point.[2]

Some of the states of Europe increased their revenues dramatically in the seventeenth century. Others suffered a decline in income. In millions of pounds sterling the figures for the leading powers in 1715 are: France £7m.; Britain £5·5m.; Austria and the Dutch Republic £2·5m.; Russia and Spain £1·6m.; Venice, Portugal and Turkey £1·3m.; Prussia £1·2m.[3] Austria's revenue derived in roughly equal proportions from Austro-Hungary, Belgium, Milan and Naples: i.e. it had quadrupled as a result of the War of Spanish Succession. The Dutch continued to have the highest *per capita* yield but were now overstraining their resources. Though it was a tribute to the Republic's creditworthiness that it managed to raise its debt to £90 million in the course of the war, its insistence on servicing this huge sum (nearly twice the size of the British debt at the time) was to place a crippling burden on the national economy. The French came out of the war with a debt of £120 million, bigger in absolute terms but smaller in relation to resources: moreover, they cheerfully inflated away half of it in the next decade.

It will be seen that in economic terms the absolute monarchies did not shine. Louis XIV's initiatives were either abortive (like Colbert's tariffs) or irrelevant (like the tapestry and mirror factories set up to supply the royal palaces). His government was at its best in public transport: he bequeathed France the finest road-system in Europe as well as the first lock-canal of any length – the 148-mile Canal du Midi. In Russia Peter the Great forced the growth of an iron industry which quickly made the country self-supporting and was soon to be an important export earner. But the improvements imposed by autocracy did not have the self-multiplying quality that was to prove the outstanding characteristic of the English advances.

1. The Italian share of Mediterranean trade continued to fall, often catastrophically. Venetian cloth exports in 1715 were only 10 per cent of the 1600 figure.

2. Iron production in the area covered by the map had risen to about 200,000 tons: Swedish exports to 30,000 tons.

3. Multiply by 2·1 to convert to Venetian gold ducats. Comparisons with 1600 are then reasonably valid for prices were stable in the intervening century: silver was draining off to the Far East as fast as it was coming in from America.

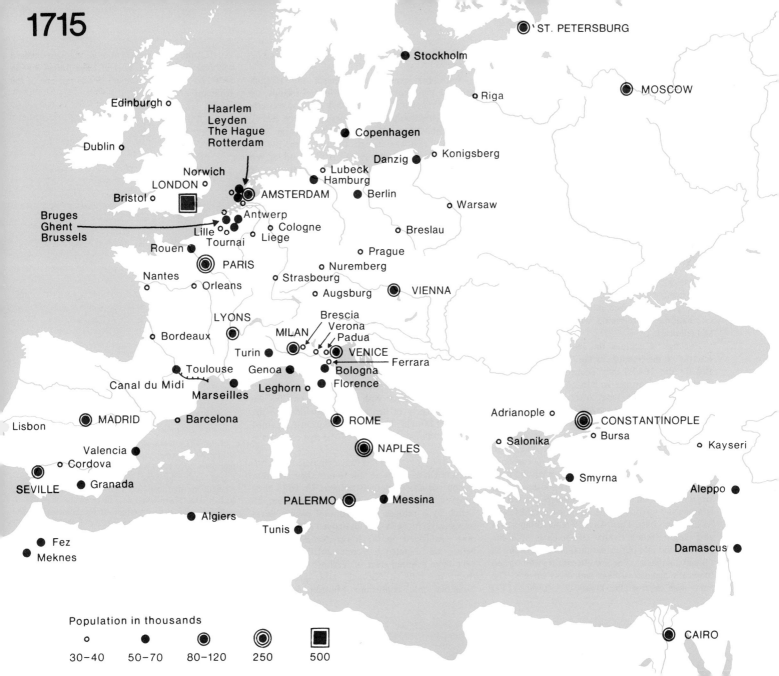

1715

St. Petersburg

Stockholm

Moscow

Riga

Edinburgh

Haarlem
Leyden
The Hague
Rotterdam

Copenhagen

Danzig

Konigsberg

Dublin

Norwich

Lubeck

Hamburg

LONDON

AMSTERDAM

Berlin

Warsaw

Bristol

Bruges
Ghent
Brussels

Antwerp

Cologne

Breslau

Lille

Liege

Tournai

Rouen

Prague

PARIS

Nuremberg

Nantes

Strasbourg

VIENNA

Orleans

Augsburg

LYONS

Brescia
Verona
Padua

Bordeaux

MILAN

Turin

VENICE

Toulouse

Genoa

Ferrara

Canal du Midi

Bologna

Marseilles

Leghorn

Florence

MADRID

Barcelona

Adrianople

CONSTANTINOPLE

Lisbon

ROME

Salonika

Bursa

Kayseri

Valencia

NAPLES

Cordova

Smyrna

SEVILLE

Granada

Aleppo

PALERMO

Messina

Algiers

Damascus

Tunis

Fez

Meknes

CAIRO

Population in thousands

30-40   50-70   80-120   250   500

The World in 1715
Political Units

In the early days of colonization every European power insisted on a legal monopoly of its colonies' trade. As none could supply a complete range of goods at competitive prices, smuggling was endemic. Attempts to supress it tended to make matters worse: the cost of coastguards had to be met from customs duties which increased the price gap between licit and illicit goods.

Spanish industry being uncompetitive, the Spanish–American economy became particularly smuggler-oriented, with smuggled goods actually exceeding official imports. More police and heavier punishments were Spain's answers, but as usual repression fought a losing battle with economics. Moreover, attacking smugglers with viciously used but basically inadequate force taught them to arm and organize themselves. The resident smugglers of the Antilles evolved into the buccaneers – an international brotherhood with its own captains and admirals.

For half a century the buccaneers were the scourge of the Spanish in the Caribbean. Originally (in the 1640s) they operated under French licence, using Tortuga, an islet off the north cost of Hispaniola, as their base. After the English took Jamaica in 1655 they moved there. It was under English patronage that the buccaneers achieved their greatest coups – including the sack of Panama in 1671 – and their decline began as soon as England decided that her Caribbean possessions were no longer in danger from Spain but did need some law and order. In the early 1680s there was a last flourish when parties of buccaneers crossed the isthmus and terrorized Spanish America's defenceless Pacific coast. Then Anglo-French disapproval and Anglo-French rivalry combined to split the brotherhood into purely national units operating as official auxiliaries. The few buccaneers who turned to piracy against all flags had short careers. The party was over: at the Treaty of Utrecht (1713)

Spain even gave the British some legal trading rights.

With the capture of Jamaica the English satisfied their appetite for Caribbean islands, as did the French in 1697 when they took the western half of Hispaniola (St Domingue, modern Haiti). The islands had only one product, sugar, and enough of this was enough. In other areas too the colonial map was steadying. At the end of the Anglo-Dutch wars the Dutch conceded the loss of New Holland in return for a free hand in Guyana: a similar division east of the Cape (which the Dutch had colonized in 1652) reserved the major share of the India trade to England, of the Indonesian to V.O.C.

The gainer from these agreements was undoubtedly England. Her North American colonists were thriving, absorbing ever more English goods: her stake in India was proving increasingly profitable. Though the Dutch remained the leaders in world trade the gap between them and the English was fast narrowing. France made a poor third: her colonists in North America were numerically weak and economically unprofitable: her trade elsewhere disrupted as a result of war with the major maritime powers.[1] At the bottom of the league was Portugal: she retained her bases in India thanks to English intercession with the Dutch, but lost the more northerly of her East African ports to the Sultan of Muscat. The arabs subsequently regained their traditional dominance of the east-coast slave trade.

By 1662 the Manchus had completed the conquest of China and were able to turn their attention to the periphery of their empire. In 1683 they annexed Formosa (which had been taken from the Dutch by a refugee Ming admiral twenty years previously). In 1686 they destroyed a Cossak outpost established on the lower Amur two years before and dictated a frontier settlement which gave them a broad tract of territory north of the river. In 1696 a Kalmuk raid threw Outer Mongolia into confusion: Manchu musketeers

expelled the raiders and Outer Mongolia became a Manchu protectorate. East of Lake Baikal Siberia now had a defined frontier: it was not one of the Russians' choosing.

1. In 1715 there were about 400,000 colonists in British North America, 20,000 in New France. The fact that their fur traders had covered the whole great lakes region encouraged the French to overestimate their strength: on the map New France looked as big as the British area. There was a notable extension of this tendency following the exploration of the Mississippi. (The upper reaches were discovered by Joliet from Lake Michigan in 1673: LaSalle sailed down the river to its mouth in 1682.) A province of Louisiana was immediately proclaimed, embracing the whole Mississippi basin. Even a generation later the only reality to this was a small settlement near the mouth of the river and a few forts upstream.

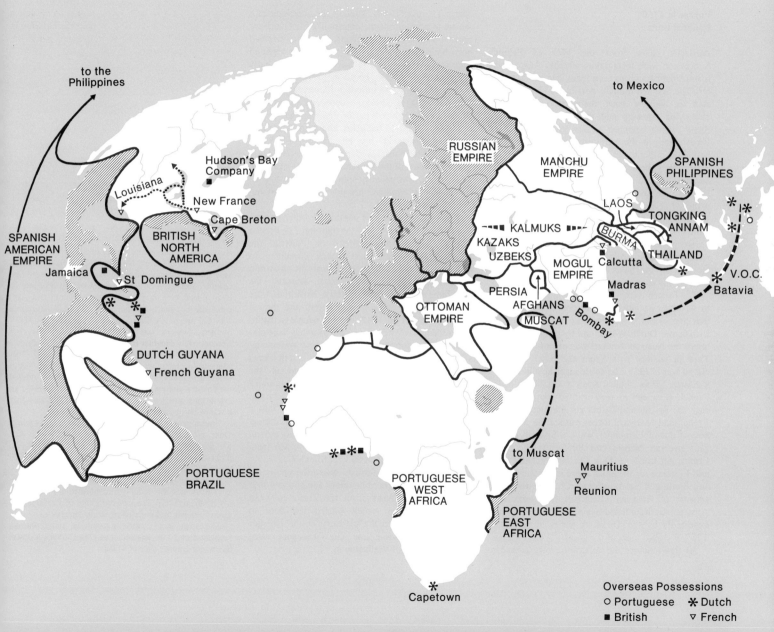

1715

to the
Philippines

Hudson's Bay
Company

Louisiana

New France

Cape Breton

BRITISH
NORTH
AMERICA

SPANISH
AMERICAN
EMPIRE

Jamaica

St Domingue

DUTCH GUYANA

▽ French Guyana

PORTUGUESE
BRAZIL

RUSSIAN
EMPIRE

MANCHU
EMPIRE

to Mexico

SPANISH
PHILIPPINES

LAOS

KALMUKS

TONGKING
ANNAM

BURMA

KAZAKS
UZBEKS

Calcutta

THAILAND

MOGUL
EMPIRE

Madras

V.O.C.
Batavia

PERSIA
AFGHANS

Bombay

OTTOMAN
EMPIRE

MUSCAT

to Muscat

Mauritius

▽ Reunion

PORTUGUESE
WEST
AFRICA

PORTUGUESE
EAST
AFRICA

* Capetown

Overseas Possessions
○ Portuguese   * Dutch
■ British   ▽ French

Europe in 1750
Political Units

Austria's gains from the War of Spanish Succession were formidable: whether Austria was formidable enough to keep them was another matter. The Spanish thought not. In 1717 they had a stab at winning back their Italian provinces, occupying Sardinia and the next year invading Sicily (which belonged to Savoy). Thanks to the British fleet in the Mediterranean the Austrians had little difficulty in beating the Spanish out of Sicily: they kept this acquisition, giving Savoy Sardinia instead (1720). Spanish pride was mollified by the promise that Don Carlos (a Spanish prince, but not in line for the throne of Spain) would get Parma and Florence when their current childless rulers died. Meantime Eugene won a crushing victory over the Turks at Peterwardein which put the Austrian frontier comfortably on the far side of the Save (1718). The new enlarged Austria had passed its first test with flying colours.

The French took little pleasure in this and began to build up an anti-Austrian coalition. They saw that the essential requirement was to keep the British and Dutch neutral and by promising not to touch the Austrian Netherlands managed to do so. Then in alliance with Spain and Savoy they declared war (1733). The subsequent hostilities were a disaster for an isolated Austria. On the Rhine the French advanced as they wanted (not too far in case the British and Dutch got alarmed): in Italy French and Savoyard forces pushed the Austrians almost out of Lombardy while a Spanish contingent overran Naples and Sicily. At the peace France got Lorraine, Don Carlos swapped Parma and Florence for the much more important Naples and Sicily and Savoy advanced her border at the expense of Austrian Milan.[1] A few years later Austria was humiliated again, this time quite unexpectedly by the Turks. A series of defeats in 1737–9 erased most of the gains of Peterwardein.

At this juncture the Austrian crown passed to Maria Theresa (1740). Though the accession of a female to a conglomerate empire like the Hapsburg created a lot of legal problems, the difficulties had been long foreseen and Maria Theresa's right to succeed acknowledged in advance by practically every state in Europe. To no major power did the pretext appear worth utilizing. However, the same year that Maria Theresa succeeded in Austria, Frederick II became King of Prussia. Determined to make full use of the army and war chest painstakingly collected by his father, Frederick marched into Austrian Silesia and declared the province a part of the Prussian state. The legal case he advanced was patently spurious: the victory his troops won at Mollwitz provided a more convincing argument.

Following Frederick's gambit the other powers were gradually drawn into the fighting. The French supported a Bavarian attack on Austria, the British, Hanoverians and Dutch combined to oppose a French advance against the Austrian Netherlands. Spain and France attacked the Austrians and Savoyards in Italy. Hostilities were somewhat desultory and intermittent and though the war went on till 1748 the only people to distinguish themselves were France's Marshal Saxe and Prussia's Frederick. Saxe won some convincing victories over the Anglo-Hanoverian-Dutch forces and ultimately conquered the whole of the Austrian Netherlands. Frederick, whose military career had got off to an undistinguished start at Mollwitz (where he ran away), developed into a skilful tactician – aggressive and quick-thinking. When the fighting was over he was the only person to show a profit, for though all other pre-war frontiers were restored, Prussia kept Silesia.[2]

Provoked by a foolish Swedish coup the Russians took another bite out of Finland in 1743: they had taken Azov from the Turks in 1736 (during the war in which Austria had done so badly) and annexed the territory of the Dnieper Cossacks at the same time. The Turks suppressed the principality of Wallachia in 1716.

1. This war is called the War of Polish (sic) Succession. The story goes like this. Ever since the Russians had restored the Elector of Saxony to the Polish throne during the Great Northern War, Poland had been near enough a Russian satellite. This situation most Poles resented and when in 1733 the nobles had a chance to elect a new king they chose not the Saxon (Russian) candidate but the native-born Leszczynski – the same who had previously been puppet king for Charles XII of Sweden. Sweden was out of the game now, but Leszczynski's daughter had married Louis XV of France so there were great hopes that the French would effectively support the independence movement. This was to ignore geography. The next year a Russian army entered the country and called a new election which revealed an astonishing swing to the Saxon candidate. He was duly installed on the throne.

France saved face by making the fugitive Leszczynski Duke of Lorraine. This tied the eastern hostilities in with the western and allows the three wars of 1701–13, 1731–5 and 1740–8 to have artificially matching titles – Spanish, Polish and Austrian Succession.

Because of Leszczynski's term as Duke of Lorraine, the Duchy was not officially incorporated in France until his death in 1766. The original Duke of Lorraine was given Florence and married to Maria Theresa.

2. Austria lost a little ground in Italy: Parma, recovered in 1738, was ceded to Don Carlos's brother; Savoy got another slice of Milan.

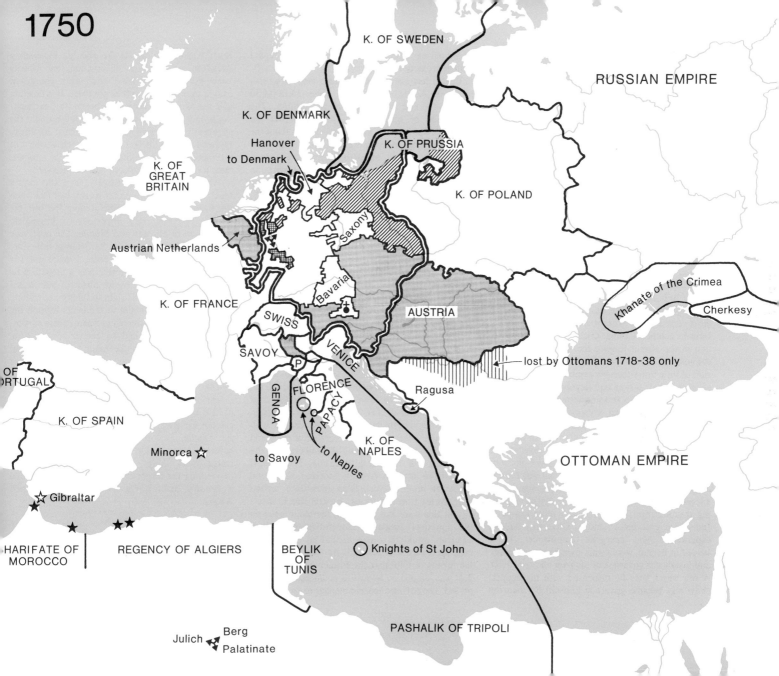

1750

RUSSIAN EMPIRE

K. OF SWEDEN

K. OF DENMARK

Hanover to Denmark

K. OF PRUSSIA

K. OF GREAT BRITAIN

K. OF POLAND

Austrian Netherlands

Saxony

Khanate of the Crimea

Cherkesy

Bavaria

K. OF FRANCE

AUSTRIA

SWISS

SAVOY

VENICE

lost by Ottomans 1718-38 only

P

Ragusa

GENOA

FLORENCE

PAPACY

OF PORTUGAL

K. OF SPAIN

to Savoy

to Naples

K. OF NAPLES

OTTOMAN EMPIRE

Minorca ☆

Gibraltar ☆
★

★

★★

HARIFATE OF MOROCCO

REGENCY OF ALGIERS

BEYLIK OF TUNIS

○ Knights of St John

Julich ➤➤ Berg

Palatinate

PASHALIK OF TRIPOLI

The World in 1763
Political Units

The commercial health of Britain had so obviously bloomed during the long struggle with Louis XIV and that of its enemies – and allies – so obviously declined that it is surprising to find the peace party firmly in control of the country for the next generation. In fact, it was not until 1739 that the militants managed to engineer a war with Spain: this was only a little in advance of the general European conflict of the 1740s – the War of Austrian Succession – of which it soon became a part. Belligerence proved disappointing. The British war machine had got more than a little rusty since Marlborough's day and Britain's main opponent, France, proved capable of a successful holding operation overseas while making good progress on the continent of Europe.

The next round – the Seven Years War – followed on shortly. The first decision came in the most remote of the areas where French and British were in conflict – India. Owing to the fragmentation of the Mogul Empire the situation there was complicated. The Mogul Emperor was in possession of little more than his capital of Delhi and not always of that: power had devolved on the governors of the northern and southern provinces (Oudh and Bengal: Hyderabad, Mysore and the Carnatic), with the Hindu Marathas taking the territory in between. The British and French had so far confined themselves to taking different sides in the disputes that arose round these shaky thrones. Then in 1756 the governor of Bengal was foolish enough to storm the British post at Calcutta. It was a totally mistimed provocation: the British, expecting trouble from the French, had more troops in India than ever before and in Clive they had an experienced and energetic commander. Clive landed in Bengal, won a walk-over battle at Plassey and installed a governor of his own choice (1757). A few years later he dispensed with the puppet-show and became governor himself. By then the

neighbouring province of Oudh had accepted British protection.

Bengal has always been India's most populous province. At this time it had some 35,000,000 inhabitants and a revenue of £2 million. The acquisition of resources on this scale put the British power in India in a different class from the French, whose enclaves were consequently soon eliminated. Indeed, the Bengal treasury proved adequate for the task on which the next generation of British nabobs embarked – the conquest of the whole subcontinent.

In other theatres the British got off to a shakier start. However, as the Royal Navy tightened its blockade of France's Atlantic ports, French overseas strength wilted. In 1759 a British expedition sailed up the St Lawrence and took Quebec, the heart of French North America. Other expeditions picked off France's Caribbean islands and West African slaving posts. Piece by piece the French colonial Empire was being removed from the board.

To the strategists in Paris there seemed only one counter to Britain's victorious progress overseas: an invasion of the British Isles. The essential preliminary was a successful fleet action, but as no one believed the French navy could beat the British the planners decided to leave this problem for later and get down to details. The result was a fantasy. The Mediterranean fleet was to rendezvous with the Atlantic fleet at Brest. Together they would pick up an army assembling at Quiberon on the south coast of the Brest peninsula. They would deposit this army in Western Scotland, sail round the north of the British Isles, pick up a second army in the Low Countries (Austria was France's ally in this war) and land this, the main force, in the south of England. Hopefully, the British admirals would be a step behind all the way. In fact, they were a step ahead. As soon as it got to the Straits of Gibraltar the French Mediterranean fleet was jumped by its British counterpart and dispersed. The Atlantic fleet did manage to escape from

Brest when Admiral Hawke and his blockading squadron were blown off position, but Hawke knew exactly where the French were going and caught up with them as they got there. In a howling gale the two fleets entered Quiberon Bay, exchanging broadsides as they went. Nightfall brought the apparently indecisive action to a halt: daybreak revealed the total defeat of the French. A third of their ships were write-offs in one way or another, the survivors were scattered and demoralized.

After Quiberon the Royal Navy did pretty much as it wished around the world. In 1762 when the French talked Spain into joining the war the British response was imperious – immediate occupation of Havana and Manila. The next year peace was signed on terms that showed how one-sided the war at sea had been. France got her Caribbean islands back (there was a limit to how much sugar Britain could absorb) but ceded Canada and gave up the right to fortify her trading posts in India. Her claim to the lands beyond the Mississippi was transferred to Spain. Spain surrendered Florida and had to recognize the little British settlements on the main land of Central America – in Honduras and on the Mosquito Coast. Rule Britannia.

The Chinese empire reached its maximum extent in this period with the annexation of Tibet (1720) and Chinese Turkestan (1755–9). At the eastern extremity of Asia the Russians employed the Danish explorer Bering to reconnoitre the route to America. On his first voyage he demonstrated that there was no land connection (something the forgotten Deshnev had determined a century before). On his second he reached Alaska.

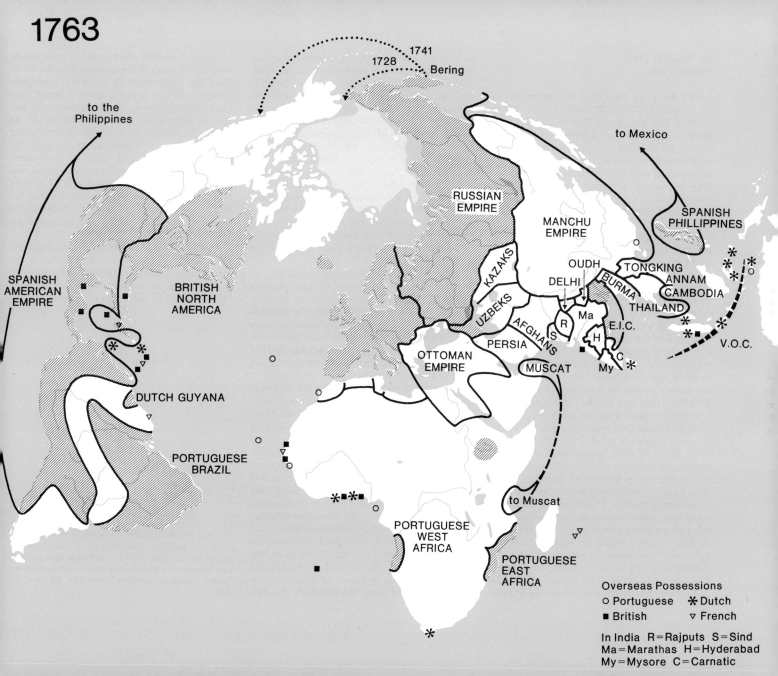

1763

1741

1728 → Bering

to the Philippines

to Mexico

SPANISH PHILLIPPINES

RUSSIAN EMPIRE

MANCHU EMPIRE

SPANISH AMERICAN EMPIRE

BRITISH NORTH AMERICA

KAZAKS

OUDH

TONGKING

DELHI

BURMA

ANNAM

CAMBODIA

UZBEKS

R   Ma

THAILAND

AFGHANS

S

E.I.C.

PERSIA

H

DUTCH GUYANA

OTTOMAN EMPIRE

C

MUSCAT

My

V.O.C.

PORTUGUESE BRAZIL

to Muscat

PORTUGUESE WEST AFRICA

PORTUGUESE EAST AFRICA

Overseas Possessions

○ Portuguese   ✳ Dutch

■ British   ▽ French

In India R=Rajputs S=Sind
Ma=Marathas H=Hyderabad
My=Mysore C=Carnatic

The World in 1783
Political Units

During the Seven Years War the cost of driving the French and Spanish from Atlantic North America was met by the British taxpayer. The colonists contributed not a penny. At the end of the war the home government, coming under the usual pressure to reduce expenditure, decided that the time had come for the Americans to pay for their own defence. The money was to be raised by a stamp duty on legal transactions such as already existed in England. The colonists decided they were having none of this. They argued that the London Parliament could legislate for them but not tax them – an interesting but quite impractical theory of partial sovereignty. They demonstrated vigorously. The British government, recognizing its inability to force the issue, took only a few months to change its mind and drop the whole idea (1765–6).

The truth was that the colonies had grown up. While the British flattered themselves that it was their military operations that had freed the colonists from the threat of conquest by Indian, Spaniard and Frenchman, steady multiplication had already carried the Americans to a numerical level where they were beyond threatening.

For a few years after the stamp duty controversy the situation was reasonably calm: the colonists were apparently satisfied with the occasional demo and a *de facto* independence; the mother country was too aware of the economic advantages of a captive market to insist on more than tokens of its *de iure* rights. Then, provoked by the British government's grant of a tea-importing monopoly to the East India Company, the radicals among the colonists organized a tea boycott. This was an immediate success: indeed in New England the authorities lost power so completely that the radicals were able to take over the Boston waterfront and dump the tea in the harbour (1773). The episode clearly demonstrated that in New England

at least the great majority of colonists now conceived of themselves as politically sovereign. Skirmishes between British troops and local militia in and around Boston provided the stimulus for the formal Declaration of Independence of 1776.

A small war ensued. The Americans could not contest control of the sea because they had no battleships: consequently they could not stop the British landing wherever they wished. On the other hand the British could not conceivably send or supply armies large enough to attempt the conquest of America. Maintaining some isolated garrisons which made occasional forays into the interior was a particularly pointless sort of war effort but one that was insufficiently exhausting to the British exchequer to provide an incentive to negotiations for peace.

Then in 1781 a French fleet acted with an American land army to compel the surrender of a British force at Yorktown, Virginia. In the sense that this brought home to the British the hopelessness of the whole business the Yorktown campaign was decisive. Over the next two years the remaining British garrisons were evacuated and in 1783 peace formally signed between the British Empire and the American Republic.

France acted with vigour during the American War of Independence. Animated by her total humiliation in the Seven Years War and freed of the continental pre-occupations that usually debilitated her global strategy, she was able to mount a more impressive naval offensive than anyone expected. Least of all the British, who in foolish overconfidence had allowed their navy to dwindle until it was little larger than the French. The British signally failed to defeat the French in the first clash of the war (Ushant, 1778): thereafter they lost their strategic grip and split the battle fleet up into separate squadrons in an attempt to protect the empire at its periphery – in India, America and the Caribbean. When the French persuaded the Spanish and Dutch to join in (1779, 1780) the British found themselves overstretched. The capi-

tulation of Yorktown was the result – and the turning point. A series of engagements gave the Royal Navy the opportunity to erode its opponents' strength, and with America tacitly dropped from strategic considerations the British admiralty was able to concentrate against the French in the Caribbean. Victory here (battle of the Saintes 1782) immediately jeopardized the few gains the French and Spanish had made. At the general peace signed the next year France regained one Caribbean island (Tobago) and a West African slavery post (St Louis) – small rewards for all her efforts. Spain got back Florida and the Mosquito Coast. All in all the British had weathered the crisis remarkably well.[1]

The Americans had achieved their independence without any sacrifice of principle. Even in the darkest days of the struggle they had refused to pay any taxes to anyone. Paper money, never redeemed, paid for the armies of the revolution.

1. The British retained Canada, whose mostly French inhabitants had shown no desire to join the American revolutionaries. After the war the British element there was strengthened by the immigration of most of the 80,000 American 'loyalists' who left the new republic.

1783

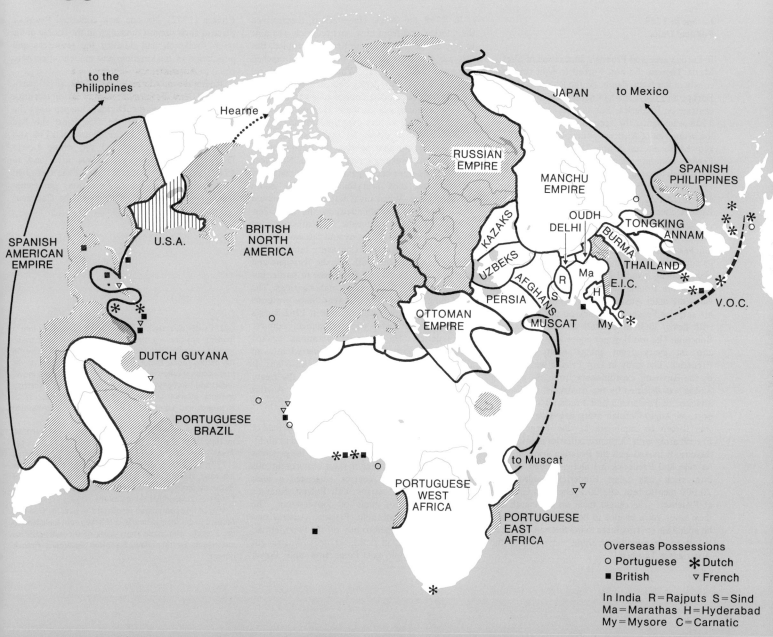

to the Philippines

Hearne

to Mexico

JAPAN

RUSSIAN EMPIRE

MANCHU EMPIRE

SPANISH PHILIPPINES

OUDH
DELHI

TONGKING
ANNAM

KAZAKS

BURMA

U.S.A.

BRITISH NORTH AMERICA

UZBEKS

R

Ma

THAILAND

E.I.C.

SPANISH AMERICAN EMPIRE

AFGHANS

PERSIA

S

H

My

C

V.O.C.

OTTOMAN EMPIRE

MUSCAT

DUTCH GUYANA

to Muscat

PORTUGUESE BRAZIL

PORTUGUESE WEST AFRICA

PORTUGUESE EAST AFRICA

Overseas Possessions

○ Portuguese   ✳ Dutch

■ British   ▽ French

In India R=Rajputs S=Sind
Ma=Marathas H=Hyderabad
My=Mysore C=Carnatic

Europe in 1783
Political Units

If Europe accepted Prussia's annexation of Silesia, Maria Theresa did not. Forced to fight simultaneously in the Netherlands, on the Rhine, in Central Europe and Italy, she had never been able to concentrate on Frederick. But as soon as the peace of 1748 was signed the recovery of Silesia became the prime aim of Austrian policy. When the British showed no interest Maria Theresa turned to the French, initiating a diplomatic revolution in which the British found themselves willy-nilly paired with Frederick (they had to have some continental ally) and Frederick found himself facing France, Austria, Sweden and Russia.

Frederick was not the man to wait on events. While Maria Theresa was still putting the finishing touches to her coalition he invaded Saxony, forced its surrender and announced its annexation (1756). Next year he invaded Bohemia, won a costly victory before Prague and had the city under siege when the main Austrian army came up. Much to his surprise Frederick's attack on this force failed with heavy loss: as a result he had to evacuate Bohemia. The war now got under way on all fronts and on every front things went badly for Frederick. The army in East Prussia was defeated by the Russians' expeditionary force, the army in Silesia was defeated by the Austrians, the Swedes attacked in Pomerania and Frederick's only support, an Anglo-German army based on Hanover, was forced to capitulate by the French. This French army with German auxiliaries now invaded Saxony. It looked as if the Prussian army had lost its *élan* and Frederick his tactical touch, but the impression was false: Frederick needed only 20,000 men to beat 60,000 French and Germans at Rossbach – he caught them on the march and they never got a chance to deploy. A month later he added his striking force to the Silesian army and led it to an equally crushing victory over the Austrians at Leuthen.[1]

In 1758 the Anglo-Hanoverians reassembled their forces and from now on Frederick was able to rely on them keeping the French occupied. But this was also the year when the Russians reached the main theatre of war. When they were thirty miles from Berlin Frederick detached himself from an inconclusive campaign in Bohemia and launched his best battalions against them. He won this battle (at Zorndorf) but victory over the Russians proved more costly than defeat by the Austrians. And worn out by constant fighting the quality of the Prussian army was beginning to decline. Next year the Russians were back again and at Kunnersdorf their squares took everything Frederick could throw at them. When night fell half the Prussian army lay dead or wounded on the field. For Frederick it was a catastrophe. In its aftermath the Austrians moved into Saxony and Silesia.

Somehow Frederick got an army into the field for the campaign of 1760. All the Russians and Austrians had to do was force him to battle, but the months passed in careful manoeuvrings. The same thing happened the next year. Some positions were won but the war was lost, for in 1762 Russia got a new tsar who was a fanatical admirer of Frederick. He ordered operations against Frederick to cease and indeed entered into an alliance with Frederick against the Austrians. It was the miracle Frederick needed. At the treaty which put an end to the Seven Years War Austria finally accepted that Silesia was part of Prussia (1763).

Frederick had fought and endured on the field of battle: he now showed himself a dab hand at diplomacy. The Austrians were alarmed by the progress the Russians were making in their near-continuous war with Turkey. Frederick suggested a joint approach to the Russians with Poland, Russia's satellite, as a good topic of conversation. The Russians could not fight Prussia, Austria and Turkey so they agreed to buy off the two German powers with slices of Polish territory. Austria got Galicia, Frederick got Pomerania and Polish

Prussia (1772). No one now contested Prussia's place at such summit meetings: in the course of his reign Frederick had doubled the resources and population of his kingdom and made it effectively equal to Austria.[2]

Russia did not do badly out of this (first) partition of Poland. Besides her slice of Polish territory (everything east of the Divina–Dnieper line) she took full advantage of the free hand she had obtained against the Turks. Between 1774 and 1783 her armies conquered the whole Lower Dnieper–Crimea–North Caucasus area and in 1783, when the most important of the Georgian principalities sought her protection, she established her first garrisons south of the Caucasus (off the map).

1. Frederick's trick was to *deploy* his army into a flanking position – a manoeuvre that demanded parade-ground perfection in drill and a measure of surprise. In the battles round Prague Frederick was too slow on the first occasion (allowing the Austrians to match his movement) and too obvious on the second (allowing Austrian spoiling attacks to disrupt his advance). Success at Rossbach and Leuthen lay in the use of the ground to conceal the approach.

2. Austria managed a few small gains on other fronts: in Italy she inherited Modena (1771); in the east the Turks yielded the Moldavian province of Bukovina (1777); in Germany when the Elector of the Palatinate inherited Bavaria she was able to annex a slice of Bavarian territory as the price of recognition (1779: Frederick stopped her taking more).

Plagued by continuous revolts in Corsica, the Genoese decided to cut their losses. In 1768 they sold the island to the French, who made short work of the independence movement. So the infant Napoleon became a French citizen.

1783

K. OF SWEDEN

RUSSIAN EMPIRE

K. OF DENMARK

K. OF GREAT BRITAIN

Hanover

DUTCH REPUBLIC

K. OF PRUSSIA

K. OF POLAND

Austrian Netherlands

Bavaria

Saxony

AUSTRIA

K. OF FRANCE

SWISS

SAVOY

VENICE

P

GENOA

FLORENCE

Ragusa

to France

PAPACY

ORTUGAL

OF

K. OF SPAIN

to Savoy

to Naples

K. OF NAPLES

OTTOMAN EMPIRE

Gibraltar

SHARIFATE OF MOROCCO

REGENCY OF ALGIERS

BEYLIK OF TUNIS

Knights of St John

PASHALIK OF TRIPOLI

By the late 1780s it was apparent that France was heading for bankruptcy. As all attempts to increase the revenue came to grief on the immunity of the nobles and clergy, the government threw its hand in and advised the King to call the States General (1788). The French equivalent of the English Parliament, the States General had last met in 1614: of its three constituent estates – nobility, clergy and people – it was the third that now proclaimed itself the National Assembly and became the government of the country (1789). Like the English House of Commons the Assembly was middle-class in composition and for a few years the country functioned on a system similar to the English. A lot got done: aristocratic and clerical privileges were abolished and the administration was re-organized, while the confiscation of church lands gave the Exchequer a shot in the arm. But the fear of aristocratic reaction reinforced by the King's blundering attempts to regain control pushed the Assembly into declaring France a republic and the emigrating nobility traitors (1792). From there the slide to a people's dictatorship was rapid as a new collapse of financial credit, the spectre of foreign intervention and the frustrations of the poor pressured the Assembly into ever more extreme measures. In 1793 the King was guillotined and Robespierre put in power by the working-class Sections (District Committees) of Paris. This second revolution was widely resented in the provinces but any attempt at disobedience was ruthlessly crushed. Year 2 of the new era saw some 40,000 executions, the vast majority of them rebel peasants. The Terror had come to save the revolution.

As the French state sank to its knees the vultures gathered. In 1792 an Austro-Prussian army marched on Paris, the French army being by then so disorganized that no one expected it to offer significant opposition. However, the French did manage a stand at Valmy, where a short cannonade proved that the Austro-Prussians would have a battle on their hands if they attacked. As this was not what they were looking for they pulled back. They had stirred up a hornets' nest. At the end of the year the French surged forward all along their eastern frontier, one army overrunning Belgium, another moving north from Alsace and clearing the left bank of the Rhine, a third occupying trans-Alpine Savoy. This onslaught by forces that had been thought incapable of defence amazed and alarmed Europe. As the French were eager to spread the gospel of revolution and were prodigal in their declarations of war, 1793 saw the formation of an anti-French coalition that included just about everyone. The English and Dutch joined the Austro-Prussians on the lower Rhine. Austria and the minor Italian states sent support to the Savoyards fighting in the Alps. Spain launched an attack across the east Pyrenees. In the course of the campaign the Coalition's armies forced the French back within their frontiers but the allies were too eager to pick up the spoils of victory to finish the job. The French armies rapidly built up again as Carnot, 'the organizer of war', supplied them with conscripts and munitions at a truly revolutionary rate. As he sent nothing else but men and guns the French had to attack to keep alive. In 1794 a second surge forward began which once again bundled the allies back behind the Rhine. This time neither the river nor the winter stopped the French. General Moreau led his cavalry across the frozen Scheldt to capture the Dutch fleet: the Dutch ashore found themselves citizens of a 'Batavian republic' allied to France and paying French taxes. Spain and Prussia left the war. Almost as discouraged, the Austrians agreed to a six-month truce on the Rhine: they kept the war going in the Italian Alps however.

By mid-1794 the Terror had burnt itself out and the Republic had come under middle-class control again. This did not mean any loss of belligerence, for the new state could function only on a war footing and its armies only in an offensive role. Nevertheless, it was an extraordinarily ambitious plan that the governing five-man Directory sent to the general in command of the Riviera front – so ambitious that the army commander, after one look at his starving levies, sent it back saying it was impossible. Let the man who dreamed it up carry it out. The Directors concurred and, at the age of twenty-six, General Bonaparte (who had endeared himself to the Directors by suppressing the Sections) was told to take command of the optimistically named Army of Italy.

He arrived to find his men creeping along the coast towards Genoa to keep themselves fed and the Austrians beginning an attack on the foremost French corps. Bonaparte immediately thrust north between the Savoyard and Austrian armies, then turned against the Savoyards and drove them back on Turin in disorder. At the end of April – Bonaparte had been in command one month – Savoy accepted an armistice and a French occupation. Turning east, Bonaparte chased the Austrians out of Milan and by June had the remnants of their army locked up in Mantua. The minor Italian states quickly offered to buy peace from the conqueror: the amounts they had to pay brought tears to their eyes.

The armistice on the Rhine expired in June: Bonaparte was relying on Moreau, who commanded the French army there, to stop the Austrians reinforcing the Italian front. However, Moreau moved slowly and when he did move, was defeated. The exhausted Army of Italy found itself facing a fresh Austrian force: after various alarms and excursions this too was shut up in Mantua. At the end of the year Bonaparte rebuffed a second relieving force: in January 1797 he destroyed this and in February received the surrender of Mantua. He then resumed his advance and was within a hundred miles of Vienna when the despairing Austrians agreed to a truce.

Bar England, all France's enemies had now been defeated. Of the victorious campaigns Bonaparte's

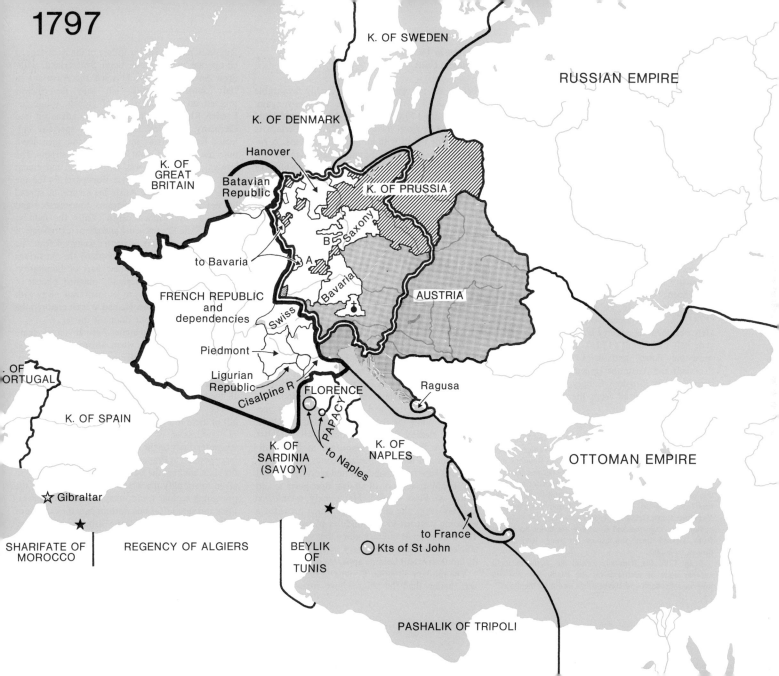

1797

K. OF SWEDEN

RUSSIAN EMPIRE

K. OF DENMARK

Hanover

K. OF GREAT BRITAIN

Batavian Republic

K. OF PRUSSIA

to Bavaria

B

Saxony

A

FRENCH REPUBLIC and dependencies

Bavaria

AUSTRIA

Swiss

Piedmont

Ligurian Republic

Cisalpine R

FLORENCE

PAPACY

Ragusa

OF ORTUGAL

K. OF SPAIN

K. OF SARDINIA (SAVOY)

to Naples

K. OF NAPLES

OTTOMAN EMPIRE

☆ Gibraltar

SHARIFATE OF MOROCCO

REGENCY OF ALGIERS

BEYLIK OF TUNIS

○ Kts of St John

to France

PASHALIK OF TRIPOLI

had undoubtedly been the most spectacular. That his success had brought him political power as well as military glory was evident in the ease with which he forced the Directory to grant him full treaty-making powers. The terms of the Peace – the creation of a French protectorate over the North Italian states (bar the eastern two-thirds of the Venetian Republic which Austria was allowed to annex) – showed that General Bonaparte was as aggressive in his politics as in his generalship. By Year 6 of the revolutionary era France was the possessor of frontiers such as her kings had always dreamed of: in the hero of the hour the revolution hailed its Caesar.[1]

The Poles had not learnt the lesson of 1774. If they were to repudiate Russia's protectorate they had to enlist the support of Prussia or Austria, preferably both. Yet they foolishly refused the Prussians' moderate price (the enclaves of Danzig and Thorn) before proclaiming a new constitution which amounted to an anti-Russian manifesto (1791–2). The Russians and Prussians immediately occupied the country and forced the Poles to cede half their lands (1793). The Poles revolted, were put down, and in 1795 the Russians, Prussians and Austrians agreed to a final dismemberment of the kingdom. Simply, and without fuss, Poland was removed from the political map of Europe.[2]

---

1. The French took trans-Alpine Savoy and Nice from the Savoyards and the Ionian Isles from Venice. Milan, Modena, the western third of the Venetian Republic and the northern quarter of the Papal States became the puppet 'Cisalpine Republic'. Genoa was transformed into the equally dependent 'Ligurian Republic'. The Swiss had lost Basle to France in 1793 and now lost the Valtelline to the Cisalpine Republic.

Batavian, Ligurian and Cisalpine are terms borrowed from classical times: the fashion for things Roman was now at its height.

2. In 1792 the Russians forced the Turks to yield another slice of territory on the Black Sea: Prussia inherited Ansbach and Bayreuth (A and B on the map).

Europe in 1803
Political Units

Before the ink was dry on the highly favourable treaties of 1797, the French were on the move again. In February 1798 they occupied the remnant Papal State and in April Switzerland. In May Bonaparte set sail for Egypt with an army of veterans. A romantic conception, the Egyptian campaign was entirely dependent on a command of the sea which the French did not have. Bonaparte got safely to Egypt (taking Malta on the way) and once there he easily defeated the Mamluks and seized the country. But then the English Mediterranean squadron under Nelson found his fleet at its anchorage in Aboukir Bay and destroyed it. Thereafter Bonaparte's activities were somewhat lacking in point: he invaded Syria, but the English supplied the Turkish garrison of Acre from the sea and he could not take it; he returned to Egypt and annihilated a Turkish force that had shipped in from Rhodes; finally he decided that France needed him and slipped off home in a fast boat (October 1799). The army he left behind surrendered to the English in 1801 (as the garrison of Malta had the year before).

France did need him. The advances of 1798 had provoked a second all-European coalition which, thanks to the Russian contingent commanded by Alexander Suvarov, had more bite than its predecessor. While the Austrians defended the Rhine, Suvarov cleared the French out of all Italy bar Genoa. A Russian fleet appeared in the Mediterranean and took the Ionian Islands. The Directory was bankrupt financially and morally and had lost its ability to control affairs: Bonaparte seized power as First Consul. He quickly established a dictatorship, the efficiency of which provided a welcome contrast to the muddles of recent years. The dedication to military glory that went with the efficiency seemed a necessary virtue at the time: its limitless extent became apparent only gradually.

The military situation Bonaparte found in 1800 was better than he might have expected. The Russians, annoyed at the failure of the Austrians to co-operate in an attack upon Switzerland, withdrew Suvarov's army. This left the Austrians in Italy somewhat weak, but they nevertheless pressed on with the siege of Genoa. While the French Rhine army under Moreau advanced into Germany, the First Consul led a specially collected Reserve Army into Switzerland, then down onto the Lombard plain behind the Austrians. The strategic conception was fine and the movement well executed, but for once Bonaparte fluffed the battle. Fearful lest the Austrians escape, he spread his net too wide: the Austrians concentrated and struck at the French centre. Only the fighting quality of the French army and the quick reflexes of its corps commanders prevented a nasty defeat. The day after the battle (at Marengo) the Austrians offered to withdraw to their part of Lombardy: Bonaparte, who had originally planned a battle of annihilation, was happy to let them walk away with their banners and guns. He had at least restored the situation in Italy in one dramatic move.

A much more convincing French victory came at the end of the year when Moreau trapped and destroyed the main Austrian army at Hohenlinden. Moreau then advanced to the gates of Vienna, the Austrian Emperor sued for peace and in 1801–2 all the belligerents came to terms.[1]

The territorial adjustments made in 1801–2 (all of them in France's favour) were followed by a re-organization of Germany in 1803. The states whose territory on the left bank of the Rhine had been incorporated in France were given compensation on the right bank: at the same time the opportunity was taken to simplify the whole jigsaw. In line with the prevailing secular trend many of these compensations and simplifications were made at the expense of ecclesiastical rulers, while the Bishopric of Salzburg (S on the map) was simply turned into a duchy.

---

1. Bonaparte never allowed Moreau another command. In 1803 he was accused of plotting against the First Consul and exiled to America.

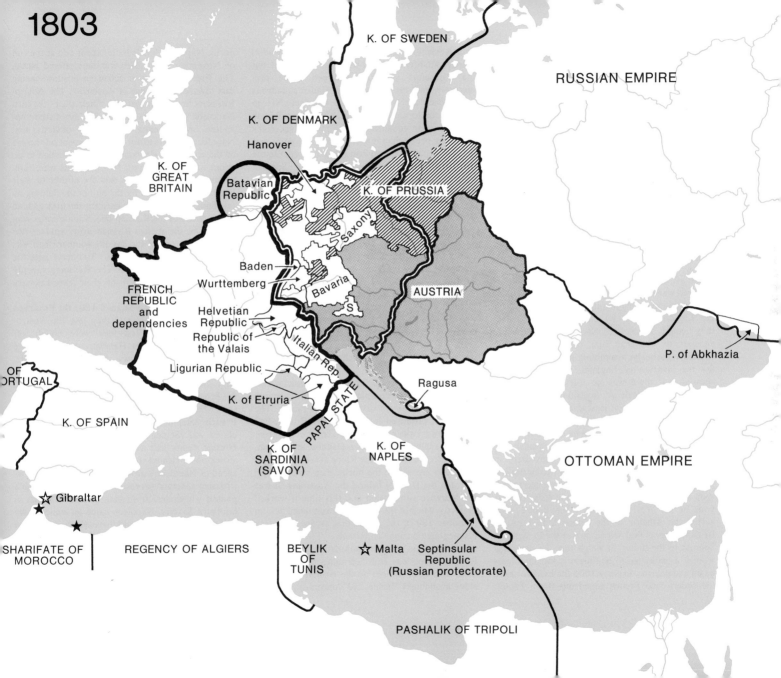

1803

K. OF SWEDEN

RUSSIAN EMPIRE

K. OF DENMARK

Hanover

K. OF
GREAT
BRITAIN

Batavian
Republic

K. OF PRUSSIA

Saxony

AUSTRIA

FRENCH
REPUBLIC
and
dependencies

Baden

Wurttemberg

Bavaria

S

Helvetian
Republic

Republic of
the Valais

Italian Rep.

Ligurian Republic

K. of Etruria

PAPAL STATE

Ragusa

P. of Abkhazia

OF
ORTUGAL

K. OF SPAIN

K. OF
SARDINIA
(SAVOY)

K. OF
NAPLES

OTTOMAN EMPIRE

☆ Gibraltar
★
★

SHARIFATE OF
MOROCCO

REGENCY OF ALGIERS

BEYLIK
OF
TUNIS

☆ Malta

Septinsular
Republic
(Russian protectorate)

PASHALIK OF TRIPOLI

Europe in 1807
Political Units

Bonaparte had seized power by *coup d'état*: his transformation into the Emperor Napoleon was by contrast unhurried and perfectly legal. If the French people hadn't actually thought of the idea they certainly liked it (plebiscite of 1804), just as they liked the return to Catholicism, law and order. The next year the Emperor turned the Italian Republic into a kingdom and crowned himself king of that; in 1806 he started handing out crowns to his family. The Royal Houses of Europe had shivered through the long night of revolution: now the sun had risen, but its light was cold and glittering.

Confident in their command of the sea, the British had no fear of Napoleon, and when he broke his promise to withdraw from Holland they declared war (1803). By close blockade of its ports they could impair the dignity, if not the strength, of the French Empire; by diplomacy and subsidy they could encourage Napoleon's continental enemies to challenge him on land. Napoleon reacted vigorously, assembling his *Grande Armée* for the invasion of England. A few rehearsals showed that there was no question of slipping across the Channel; an invasion required local control of the sea for at least a fortnight. By cajoling Spain into joining him, the Emperor obtained a fleet that was, on paper, as big as Britain's.

The trick was to concentrate the Spanish and French battleships, blockaded as they were in half a dozen different Atlantic and Mediterranean ports. Napoleon's plan called for the various squadrons to slip out of port simultaneously, rendezvous in the West Indies and then double back across the Atlantic to the Channel. Perhaps the British Channel fleet would pursue the French and Spanish to the Indies, in which case the game was won: if a battle had to be fought it should at least be on equal terms. In early 1805 the Emperor gave the order. Two French squadrons (from Toulon

and Rochefort) and one Spanish (from Cadiz) managed to break out and reach the Caribbean, but the Rochefort squadron returned home prematurely and the Toulon and Cadiz squadrons sailed back for Spain not the Channel. Nelson chased out to the West Indies with the British Mediterranean squadron, which made Napoleon's plan look better than it was: the critical point was that the British Channel fleet never budged. On the way back from the West Indies the Franco-Spanish fleet of twenty battleships was intercepted by a British fleet of fifteen. The British admiral conspicuously lacked the Nelson touch but still managed to take two of the Spaniards.

Napoleon realized that the attempt to win the Channel was hopeless and decided to try for control of the Mediterranean instead. A new series of concentrating moves was ordered. These proved successful: by August there were thirty-three French and Spanish battleships in Cadiz. In October Nelson caught them off Cape Trafalgar, where his twenty-seven ships took twenty of the enemy. The victory cost Nelson his life, but his work was done. For the rest of the war – for the rest of the century – no one challenged British sea-power again.

Two months before Trafalgar Napoleon had abandoned his invasion plans and begun to march the *Grande Armée* east across France. The Austrians, promised full support by Russia, had decided to try their luck again. They were concentrating at Ulm on the Upper Danube, and expecting the French to cross the Rhine at the same level. Napoleon crossed to the north, then swung south to reach the Danube behind the Austrians. It was the Marengo game again and this time it worked perfectly. Most of the Austrians capitulated at Ulm (October 1805): the forces that escaped the trap disintegrated during the pursuit.

At the time of the capitulation the leading Russian corps was still 100 miles to the east of Ulm. Too weak to hold up the *Grande Armée* the allies abandoned Vienna and concentrated to the

north. Napoleon hustled after them and at the end of November the Austro-Russians offered battle. The French took up a defensive position facing east towards the village of Austerlitz. The Austro-Russians formed up parallel. Their plan – to turn Napoleon's right flank and cut his line of communication with Vienna – was so obvious that Napoleon told his army what to expect on the eve of the battle. He also said what he intended to do about it. He waited until his opponents were fully committed to their attack and the middle of their line had been thinned by the pull of the fighting on this flank. Then he struck hard for the high ground in the centre of the Russian line. Soult's corps won it for him, the Austro-Russian army split in two and over the rest of the day the southern half was methodically pounded to bits.[1] Two days later the Austrians sued for peace. The Russians sullenly withdrew what was left of their expeditionary force.

Throughout the campaign of 1805 the Prussians had been dithering: should they join the Austro-Russians or not? First they were bought off by Napoleon's offer of Hanover, then they were frightened off by the news of Ulm and Austerlitz. But as Napoleon proceeded to reorganize the secondary German states according to his own ideas, the Prussians decided that they had to draw the line somewhere: rather than see Saxony become a French satellite they occupied it. Napoleon declared war (September 1806). From Austria the *Grande Armée* had withdrawn to Bavaria; now it struck north-east on the direct route to Berlin. The speed of Napoleon's advance was too much for the Prussian generals' nerves: outflanked, they began a phased withdrawal from their position at Jena in Southern Saxony. Napoleon came up while nearly half the Prussians were still there. He overwhelmed these divisions on the spot. Fifteen miles to the north, at Auerstadt, the remainder was caught by one of Napoleon's flanking corps (Davout's). It is a measure of the tactical superiority of the *Grande Armée* that Davout's 26,000 men were able to

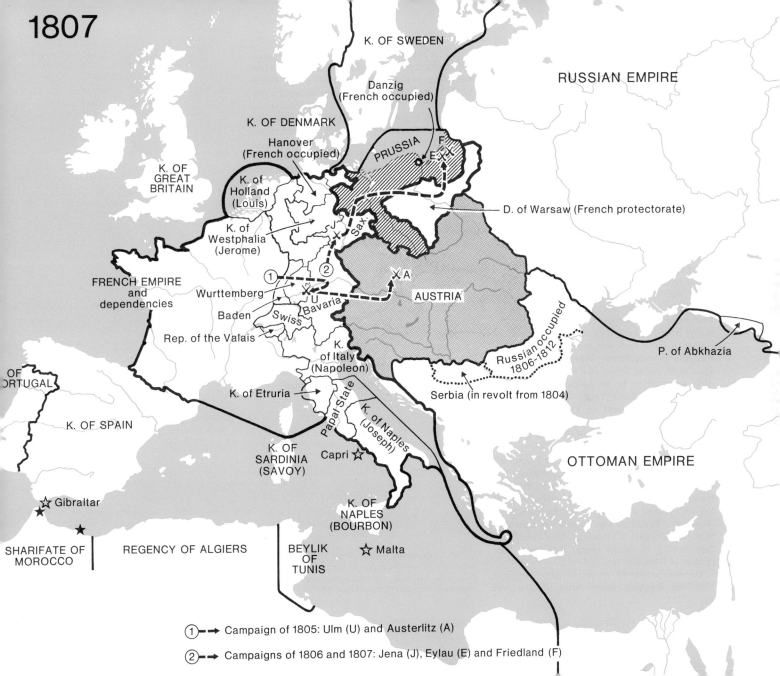

1807

K. OF SWEDEN

RUSSIAN EMPIRE

Danzig
(French occupied)

K. OF DENMARK

PRUSSIA

F.
E.

Hanover
(French occupied)

K. OF
GREAT
BRITAIN

K. of
Holland
(Louis)

D. of Warsaw (French protectorate)

K. of
Westphalia
(Jerome)

Sax.

FRENCH EMPIRE
and
dependencies

① ②

Wurttemberg

X A

Baden

U

Bavaria

AUSTRIA

Swiss

Rep. of the Valais

Russian occupied
1806-1812

K. of Italy
(Napoleon)

P. of Abkhazia

K. of Etruria

Papal State

Serbia (in revolt from 1804)

OF
PORTUGAL

K. of Naples
(Joseph)

OTTOMAN EMPIRE

K. OF SPAIN

K. OF
SARDINIA
(SAVOY)

Capri ☆

☆ Gibraltar

★

K. OF
NAPLES
(BOURBON)

SHARIFATE OF
MOROCCO

REGENCY OF ALGIERS

BEYLIK
OF
TUNIS

☆ Malta

① ➡ Campaign of 1805: Ulm (U) and Austerlitz (A)

② ➡ Campaigns of 1806 and 1807: Jena (J), Eylau (E) and Friedland (F)

attack, envelop and destroy this force of 63,000 Prussians.

The pursuit after Jena–Auerstadt was ruthless. Davout was at the gates of Berlin within ten days of the battle and the remnants of the Prussian army were expertly shepherded westward (to prevent them linking up with the Russians) and forced to surrender. The longest-lasting Prussian formation was Blücher's, which fought all the way back to Lübeck before surrendering in early November.

The King of Prussia was now without an army, but once again a Russian one was on the way. It had got as far as Warsaw. Napoleon advanced, pushed the Russians out of the Polish capital by the end of the month and was across the Vistula in force in December. Then the *Grande Armée* went into winter quarters. In January 1807 the Russians launched a surprise offensive: the French repulsed it and pursued the Russians north. The battle of Eylau was fought in a snowstorm: a combination of dogged courage and tactical luck gave the Russians a draw and the *Grande Armée* its first really heavy casualty list. It was a check to Napoleon which made him more careful – and the Russians over-confident. When fighting started again in the spring they took a chance by attacking what appeared to be an isolated French corps (Lannes') at Friedland. To do so meant offering battle with their backs to a river so that if Napoleon could get his main force there in time the attackers would be massacred. He did, and they were.

The *Grande Armée*'s sweep through Europe left Napoleon without a rival on the continent. The only power that retained the capacity to resist was Russia, and after Friedland Tsar Alexander was too discouraged to go on trying. Particularly as Napoleon offered him what looked like a partnership, gave him part of Prussia's slice of Poland and took nothing in return except the Ionian Isles (Treaty of Tilsit, 1807).

On the conquered Austrians and Prusssians Napoleon imposed pitiless terms. Austria was forced to cede the Tyrol to Bavaria and Venetia and Dalmatia to the Kingdom of Italy. Prussia lost everything west of the Elbe, most of its Polish provinces and Danzig. Danzig was declared a free city: the Polish provinces were reassembled into a Duchy of Warsaw which had the Elector of Saxony as its Grand Duke; both were simply French client-states. At the same time the Holy Roman Empire was dissolved and replaced by a 'Confederation of the Rhine' of which Napoleon was official protector. The pro-French members of the confederation were further enlarged in the reorganization.

Behind Napoleon's armies marched Napoleon's family. In 1806 the King of Naples was chased from his capital and Joseph Bonaparte established on his throne. The Batavian Republic was turned into a kingdom for brother Louis the same year. Brother Jerome was given the Kingdom of Westphalia, sister Eliza got Lucca. Also available though as yet unallotted was the crown of Portugal – the Portuguese had been so lacking in enthusiasm for the Napoleonic system that the Emperor was forced to occupy their country (1807). British sea-power preserved Sicily for the ex-King of Naples, as it had Sardinia for the ex-King of Savoy but, for the moment, could do nothing for the King of Portugal. He had to take refuge in Brazil.

1. At this time the *Grande Armée* consisted of seven consecutively numbered corps (commanded by Marshals Bernadotte, Marmont, Davout, Soult, Lannes, Ney and Augereau), the guard (Bessières) and the cavalry (Murat).

At Tilsit Napoleon had determined to be generous to his new friend the Tsar. The difficulty was to find something to be generous with, for France controlled the continent up to the Russian frontier and, of course, nothing that France controlled could be given up. Finland was available but hardly enough by itself; what about a Franco-Russian partition of the Ottoman Empire? The Russians were grateful for Finland (which they annexed in 1808–9) but cautious about Turkey. They had been making steady progress against the Ottomans on their own and were already occupying what they saw as their next slice – the Turkish provinces north of the Danube. If Napoleon talked of much more dramatic advances he was worryingly vague about where the line of division would fall. No doubt of his enthusiasm – the Egyptian campaign had only whetted his appetite for Alexander-style conquests in the East. Most certainly he had the resources to drive through Constantinople into Asia. But, Turkey conquered, would the Tsar find himself fobbed off with the promise of India?

Troubles at the other end of Europe forced Napoleon to shelve his plans for the Levant. The King of Spain was being irritating: from every point of view Joseph Bonaparte (currently King of Naples) would be a better ruler. In March 1808 French line of communication troops supplying the army of occupation in Portugal, plus a couple of corps slid into northern Spain in the guise of reinforcements, carried out a bloodless coup. In early May Marshal Murat helped the Madrid parliament discover its hitherto well-concealed yearning for Joseph. The whole operation was fast and smooth and blown to pieces by a national rising at the end of the month. Joseph arrived to find that his kingdom consisted of little more than Madrid. A British expeditionary force was liberating Portugal.

Furious, Napoleon hurried into the Peninsula with another 100,000 men. He crushed the Spaniards and chased the British out of the country (but not out of Portugal). Then he left. Two months was all he could spare for Joseph's problems, for the Austrians had decided to make another attempt to break the French grip on Europe.

The Austrian declaration of war in 1809 was the result of an upsurge of anti-French feeling similar to the Spanish fury Joseph was experiencing. On a cool analysis no one could expect the Austrian army, reformed and enlarged though it was, to defeat the much larger, perennially victorious, forces of the French Empire. Nevertheless, Napoleon was somewhat too confident. Attempting to direct the war from Paris he failed to get his army in Bavaria concentrated and nearly lost Davout's corps as a result. He arrived on the battlefield of Ratisbon in time to retrieve the situation, but it was not one of his best victories. The Austrians, bruised but intact, retired north of the Danube: the French moved along the south bank and occupied Vienna. Here, or to be exact at Aspern, five miles to the east, Napoleon decided to cross to the north bank. What he did not know was that the Austrians had kept pace with him. The first two French corps across found themselves under attack by the whole Austrian army. They held out – just – and that night Napoleon got Lannes' corps and the Guard over to join them. Davout was to follow the next day. But now came real trouble. The Austrians had been launching barges down the river in an attempt to break the French pontoon bridge. Early on the morning of the second day a big barge hit the bridge and smashed it completely. The French across the river were too weak to break out and were taking heavy casualties. Napoleon had to concede his first defeat by evacuating the bridgehead under cover of darkness.

As an army commander Napoleon might have tried a new plan; as Emperor he had to show Europe that he was unstoppable. Orders went out calling in every available man and gun and six weeks after the battle of Aspern the French army crossed again – at the same place but in twice the strength. The Austrians were in position some miles back, at Wagram. The French attacked headlong, the Austrians held and counter-attacked. When both sides were nearing exhaustion Napoleon committed his 10,000-strong reserve in the form of a huge square aimed straight at the Austrian centre. It didn't break through but it did break the Austrian commander's nerve. He ordered a retreat and advised the government to sue for peace.

The price of peace with Napoleon was, as usual, high. Austria had to cede Galicia to the Duchy of Warsaw (bar one small enclave which Napoleon gave to the Tsar as a reward for his neutrality) and Croatia to the French Empire's Illyrian province.[1]

Though Wagram was Napoleon's least elegant victory to date it impressed Europe more than any of its predecessors. Where previously there had been the hope that, with improved generalship and a bit of luck, Napoleon could be beaten, now it seemed as if his energy, his ruthlessness and his big battalions would carry him over any obstacle. The image of the great square marching relentlessly forward at Wagram created a new Napoleonic myth, not of genius but of sheer power: the trail of blood it left behind also had its effect on French attitudes towards their Emperor.

The war went on. The only contestants left in the ring now were France and Britain. The Duke of Wellington was holding Portugal against the best of Napoleon's marshals, which annoyed the Emperor but did not worry him. The main consequence of Franco-British belligerence was mutual blockade. For various reasons Napoleon got less from his counter-blockade than he expected: it also forced him to coerce his satellites mercilessly. In 1810 he annexed Holland because brother Louis was not enforcing the embargoes. He then carried the annexation up to the root of Denmark so as to seal off the trade of Germany. More important, he took umbrage when Tsar Alexander decided to resume trade with Britain. No one could remain independent of the Napoleonic system. He began to plan the invasion of Russia. The scale of the preparations was in itself intoxicating. In June 1812 he deployed half a million men (half of them French) on Poland's eastern frontier.

The Russians steadily retreated before the main thrust, which took Napoleon and 200,000 men on the direct route to Moscow. They made a stand at Borodino, seventy miles in front of the city, but Napoleon bludgeoned them out of position in a Wagram-type battle. He entered Moscow at the head of 100,000 men in mid-September. Alexander stuck to his decision not to negotiate while the French were on Russian soil: Napoleon found himself with no meaningful move to make. He decided to retreat and try again – with St Petersburg the objective – next year. The rearguard left Moscow at the end of October: the Russian winter started a few days later. By the time the French reached Smolensk their condition was critical: horses and men were starving, effective strength down to 50,000. Russian forces twice as large were on their flanks. Napoleon managed to cut his way out and see what was left of the army across the Beresina, the last physical barrier on the line of retreat. Then in early December he left for Paris to raise reinforcements. The shattered regiments he left behind could not prevent the Russians liberating Prussia (March 1813).

Napoleon raised his new army and rushed it to Saxony. For a moment he seemed to have recovered his old skill; he beat back the Russians and Prussians and when the Austrians finally made up their minds to join the coalition against him he bloodied their noses in quite the old style at Dresden. But his raw recruits could not stand the pace; his marshals were old and the allies dogged. Gradually he was crowded back into Leipzig. The evacuation of the city – a serious defeat in itself – became a disaster when the only bridge was blown prematurely, leaving a quarter of the French army to be captured. 'The Battle of the Nations', as Leipzig was termed, was not as impressive in terms

78

of generalship but it was decisive. In the campaign of 1814 Napoleon displayed demoniac energy but could not stop the allies converging on Paris. He abdicated in exchange for the principality of Elba.

The allies decided to restore the Bourbon line (in the person of Louis XVIII) to the French throne: they were still discussing the new frontiers Europe was to have when Napoleon escaped from Elba and landed in the south of France (February/March 1815). The French were not yet ready to abandon the dream of empire, the veterans of the *Grande Armée* had no wish for peace. The King fled, the Emperor was restored. Napoleon promised a constitutional empire in place of the dictatorship he had wielded before, he promised peace. But the allies would not receive his soft words and immediately declared war.

The Russians had a long way to come and the Austrians never got anywhere fast. The British and Prussians poured everything they could raise into Belgium: their armies (under Wellington and Blücher) were the ones Napoleon had to destroy. Sixty days after he had landed in the south, forty days after he had arrived in Paris, the Emperor was on the Belgian frontier with 150,000 men. The allies, their armies ten miles apart, had no idea he was anywhere near; Napoleon had the advantage he needed. While Ney, with the left wing, held off the British at Quatre Bras, the Emperor trounced the Prussians at Ligny. Wellington and Blücher were forced to retreat by parallel roads to Brussels. Napoleon transferred his main force to the British front. The allies were still almost ten miles apart, but on Blücher's assurance that he could get to him if he was attacked, Wellington decided to stand at Waterloo. Napoleon's assault was frontal and a bloody failure. When Blücher finally came up (very late) the French withdrawal turned into a rout. His army destroyed, Napoleon returned to Paris and abdicated again. The Hundred Days were over. This time there was no little principality: he was imprisoned on the island of St Helena in the south Atlantic.[2]

1. The creation of this province reflects Napoleon's continuing interest in Turkey, as does the trouble he went to to maintain French garrisons in the Ionian Isles.

2. Of the nine marshals enumerated in the footnote on p. 76, Lannes was killed at Aspern and Bessières in the opening phase of the Leipzig campaign. Murat, who succeeded Joseph as King of Naples, was deposed and executed during the Hundred Days. Bernadotte was adopted by the childless king of Sweden in 1810, and as Crown Prince of Sweden fought against Napoleon in 1813: he became King of Sweden five years later.

The remaining five were retained by Louis XVIII but except for Marmont went over to Napoleon during the Hundred Days. After it was all over Davout, Soult and Augereau were disgraced; Ney was tried and shot.

1812

K. OF SWEDEN

RUSSIAN EMPIRE

Danzig (French occupied)

K. OF DENMARK

PRUSSIA

D. of Warsaw (French protectorate)

K. OF GREAT BRITAIN

K. of Westphalia (Jerome)

Saxony

Wurttemberg

Baden

Bavaria

AUSTRIA

FRENCH EMPIRE and dependencies

Swiss

K. of Italy (Napoleon)

(direct French rule)

Serbia (in revolt 1804-1813)

OF ORTUGAL

K. of Spain (Joseph)

K. OF SARDINIA (SAVOY)

K. of Naples

OTTOMAN EMPIRE

☆ Gibraltar
★

★

K. OF NAPLES (BOURBON)

British occupied

SHARIFATE OF MOROCCO

REGENCY OF ALGIERS

BEYLIK OF TUNIS

☆ Malta

PASHALIK OF TRIPOLI

- - - ➤ Napoleons march to Moscow 1812

Europe in 1815
1. Political Units

The allies who had triumphed over Napoleon in 1814 met at Vienna later the same year to recast the frontiers of Europe. Whatever was proclaimed in the way of principle – and the assembled kings and emperors were naturally strong for hereditary rights – the major powers were going to get major rewards. And Russia, the biggest of all, was to get most. However, as all three of Russia's neighbours were members of the Grand Alliance they had to be compensated on their other frontiers for Russia's gains at their expense. The end result of the Congress of Vienna was therefore a westward shift in boundaries. Russia kept Finland and increased her share of Poland. Sweden was given Norway. Prussia, besides a third of Saxony, obtained a huge 'Rhine province' that made her the predominant power in north-west Germany.

Austria's reward lay in Northern Italy. The restitution of Milan and Mantua and the addition of Venice gave the Hapsburg Empire a useful and contiguous bloc of territory embracing two thirds of the Po valley. As Florence was once again to be ruled by a Hapsburg prince, and Parma was allotted to a Hapsburg princess (specifically to Marie Louise, Napoleon's second Empress), Italy emerged from the Congress of Vienna as Austria's 'sphere of influence'.

One victor, Britain, had no continental ambitions, and took nothing in Europe except some offshore islands – Heligoland in the North Sea, Malta and the Ionian islands in the Mediterranean – to serve as bases for her sea-power.[1] The loser, France, found herself with her 1792 frontiers, minus a few border fortresses that were taken away as a punishment for the Hundred Days.

Belgium proved a problem. A small, half-French country sitting on France's doorstep, it could hardly be expected to survive France's future revival if given its independence. Yet the Austrians, who had learnt the hard way that isolated territories brought more trouble than revenue, had no interest in resuming sovereignty. The solution was to merge Belgium and the Dutch Republic into the 'Kingdom of Holland'. As its title suggests, the Dutch provided this new state with its dynasty and dominated its affairs.

As well as readjusting the power blocs of Europe the Congress of Vienna continued the process of simplifying the map of Europe. Savoy swallowed up Genoa, Prussia the final morsel of Swedish Pomerania. The secondary states of Germany were consolidated so that only the centre of the country remained in the traditional Ruritanian patchwork.

By its own standards the Congress of Vienna did a good job. The whole thing was *realpolitik*, and bad luck on the Poles and others whose national aspirations were ignored, but with some exceptions the settlement was one Europe could live with. The Belgians soon refused to put up with the Dutch as rulers and proclaimed a surprisingly successful British-guaranteed independence in 1838: the Norwegians felt the same about the Swedes but didn't get their freedom till 1902. The only other significant changes before the outbreak of the First World War in 1914 were the unification of Italy by the House of Savoy and the unification of Germany (bar Austria) by Prussia. Neither process could possibly have been anticipated by the peacemakers of 1814.

The Ottoman Empire entered the nineteenth century well rehearsed for its role as 'the sick man of Europe'. Handed back Egypt on a platter the Sultan proved unable to keep it. The governor he appointed, Mohammed Ali, quickly made himself independent in all but name and by 1822 had expanded the area under his control to include the Sudan and nearer Arabia. On the other hand Napoleon's invasion of Russia brought relief to Turkey-in-Europe. The Russians withdrew their armies from the Danube and in 1812 the Sultan was able to recover Wallachia and Moldavia (bar the Moldavian province of Bessarabia). He also obtained a free hand against the Serbs, whose revolt was suppressed the next year. Once recovered, Serbia was granted near-autonomy: it was obviously better for Turkey to have vassal states on its northern frontier than discontented peoples looking to Russia or Austria. Greek independence was more hardly won: the successful rising of 1821 was soon jeopardized by civil war and only the intervention of the European powers forced a settlement in Greece's favour ten years later. The Sultan had to recognize the autonomy of Wallachia and Moldavia at the same time: after the Crimean war they were to unite as the Kingdom of Rumania. To Serbia, Greece and Rumania were eventually added Bulgaria (1878) and Albania (1912): the nineteenth-century process of balkanization reflects the failure of Russia and Austria to press home their eighteenth-century advantage, and the assumption of responsibility for supervising Turkey's decline by the European powers in concert.

1. The British kept hoping that the connection with Hanover (which the Congress elevated into a kingdom) would lapse. Thanks to the German rule of male succession it did so on the accession of Victoria in 1837.

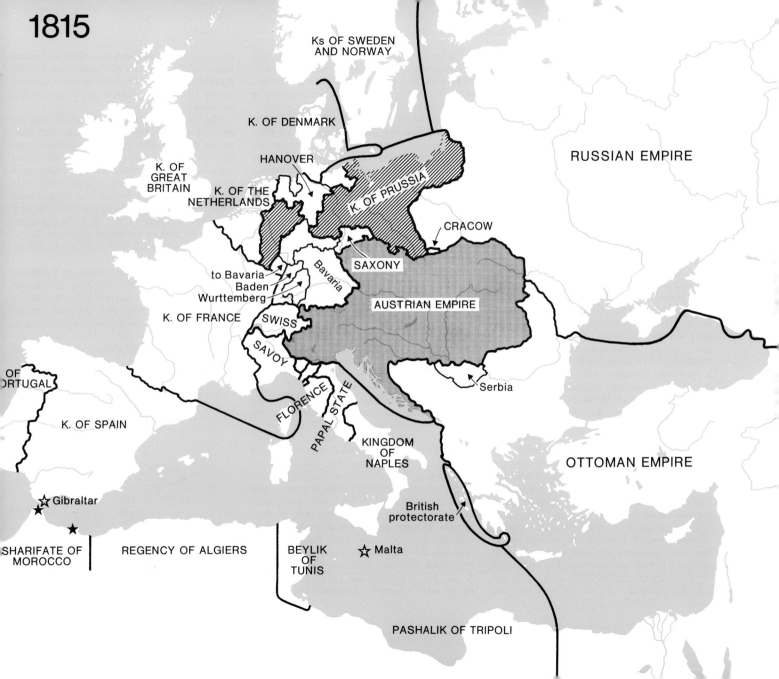

1815

Ks OF SWEDEN
AND NORWAY

RUSSIAN EMPIRE

K. OF DENMARK

HANOVER

K. OF
GREAT
BRITAIN

K. OF THE
NETHERLANDS

K. OF PRUSSIA

CRACOW

SAXONY

AUSTRIAN EMPIRE

to Bavaria
Baden
Wurttemberg

Bavaria

K. OF FRANCE

SWISS

Serbia

SAVOY

FLORENCE

PAPAL STATE

OF
RTUGAL

K. OF SPAIN

KINGDOM
OF
NAPLES

OTTOMAN EMPIRE

British
protectorate

Gibraltar

SHARIFATE OF
MOROCCO

REGENCY OF ALGIERS

BEYLIK
OF
TUNIS

Malta

PASHALIK OF TRIPOLI

The World in 1815
1. Political Units

In retrospect the Napoleonic adventure in France seems surprisingly devoid of permanent political effects: the map of Europe is not all that different before and after. But there is no denying the importance of the Napoleonic wars to the rest of the world. France's total preoccupation with Europe – a preoccupation reinforced by British blockade – allowed not only her own but her satellites' overseas empires to crumble away. The French half of San Domingo succumbed to a slave revolt and evolved into the black state of Haiti: the other French and Dutch islands in the Caribbean were taken by the British, as were their positions in Guyana. Spain's American Empire suffered even more dramatically; to the British it lost only Trinidad but, when Napoleon deposed the Spanish King in favour of Joseph Bonaparte, the hitherto obedient provinces of the Spanish Main began to set up governments of their own. First to break away was the Viceroyalty of the Rio Plata which split into the independent states of Argentina, Paraguay and Uruguay (1810–15). To the north, in Peru, New Granada and Venezuela, the wave of revolts was put down by loyalist troops, and 1815 saw the rebel leader Simon Bolivar in exile in Jamaica. But two years later Bolivar returned to the mainland and began the final liberation of the whole area. When in 1822 he and San Martin (the Argentinian who had liberated Chile) met in Peru the last pages were being written in the history of an empire that had no history except its beginning and its end. Mexico and 'Guatemala' (meaning all Central America) declared their independence in the same decade.

Incorporation in the Napoleonic system was as disastrous for the Dutch as the Spanish: besides their minor possessions in the Caribbean they lost the Cape, Ceylon and Indonesia. The British kept the Cape, Ceylon and half Guyana (paying £6 million compensation) and though they returned Indonesia the boundary between the two spheres of influence, which had been at the entry to the Straits of Malacca, was shifted to the British advantage. When the agreement was finally completed in 1822, Malaya had become a British protectorate.

Britain was obviously the beneficiary of her sea-power and Napoleon's lack of interest in his allies' overseas possessions. Even more so was the American Republic. Napoleon forced Spain to return Louisiana to France (in 1800, for nothing), then sold it to the United States (in 1803 for £6 million – $27m.). This gave the United States a vast new territory and an indefinite western frontier. President Jefferson was quick to seize the opportunity of claiming a seaboard on the Pacific: he mounted the well-organized expedition of Lewis and Clark which found a way through the Rockies in 1805 and established an American presence in the area. They were not the first across the mountain barrier. To their south the Spanish had opened the Santa Fe trail to their missions in California as early as 1774. To their north the Scot Mackenzie had crossed the Canadian Rockies in the latitude of Vancouver in 1793.[1] As the Russians were moving south from their seal-hunting grounds in Alaska it was certainly time for the Americans to stake their claim.

Of more immediate consequence for the Americans than the opening of the west was the burst of prosperity which the British blockade of the Napoleonic Empire brought to the young republic. Economically independence had not been a great success for the Americans, who had found themselves excluded from the most important mercantile network in existence. Now as neutrals they could almost monopolize trade with beleaguered Europe, bringing in not only American produce but the produce of the whole world. Exports boomed, re-exports rose even faster and the American merchant marine underwent a staggering growth. Inevitably there was friction with the British and eventually war (1812–14). But the British were reluctant combatants and the war party in America was soon discredited by the total failure of the invasions of Canada and Florida. Against expectations the resulting peace was kept: against all prediction Canada was to develop into an independent nation.

The exploration of North-West America left only Africa as a blank on the map. Even here, despite the inhabitants' poverty and the consequent lack of economic incentive, despite the killing diseases, European expeditions were beginning to investigate. De Lacerda, an unusually enterprising Portuguese who had dreams of a coast-to-coast empire in the south, tried to cross the continent first from the west (1787), then from the east (1798). He died on his second expedition. So did the Scot Mungo Park, first European to sail the Niger.

War in Europe did not prevent the Europeans from encroaching further on Asia. The British steadily extended their power in India: the effective limits of their rule were now the Indus and the Himalayas. The Russians absorbed the nearer parts of Kazakstan and enlarged their trans-Caucasian territory by annexation of Georgian principalities, repression of the local Moslem lords and some easy victories over Persia (1804–13).

1. Four years earlier Mackenzie had made an epic voyage down the river now named after him to the Arctic Ocean.

1815

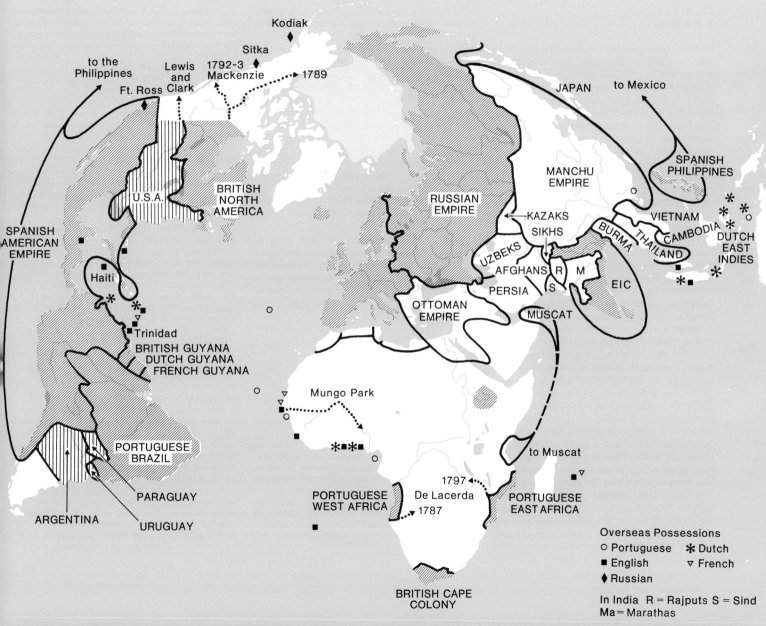

to the Philippines

Kodiak

Sitka
1792-3

Lewis
and
Clark

Mackenzie

1789

to Mexico

JAPAN

Ft. Ross

MANCHU
EMPIRE

RUSSIAN
EMPIRE

U.S.A.

BRITISH
NORTH
AMERICA

SPANISH
PHILIPPINES

SPANISH
AMERICAN
EMPIRE

KAZAKS

SIKHS

VIETNAM

Haiti

BURMA

CAMBODIA

THAILAND

DUTCH
EAST
INDIES

UZBEKS

AFGHANS

R

M

Trinidad

PERSIA

S

EIC

BRITISH GUYANA
DUTCH GUYANA
FRENCH GUYANA

OTTOMAN
EMPIRE

MUSCAT

PORTUGUESE
BRAZIL

Mungo Park

to Muscat

PARAGUAY

ARGENTINA

URUGUAY

PORTUGUESE
WEST AFRICA

1797
De Lacerda
1787

PORTUGUESE
EAST AFRICA

Overseas Possessions
○ Portuguese   ✳ Dutch
■ English   ▽ French
♦ Russian

BRITISH CAPE
COLONY

In India R = Rajputs S = Sind
Ma = Marathas

The World in 1815
2. Population

Between 1648 and 1815 the world's population rose from about 525 million to something over 900 million – a 75 per cent increase. This was three times the growth rate of the preceding period (1483–1648). Mankind was rumbling towards the population explosion of the twentieth century.

Colonization of new lands was one of the factors involved in this rapid growth. This is most obviously true where the growth rate was highest, in North America. There the immigration of skilled farmers and their unchecked natural multiplication were between them doubling the population every quarter century. From 250,000 in 1700 the white population of North America rose to 4 million in 1800 and had reached 7 million by 1815. The Negro slave population increased in parallel from 20,000 in 1700 to half a million in 1775 and 1·5 million in 1815. Add something under 1 million for the Amerindians outside the colonized area and a third of a million for the Canadians and the North American total for 1815 passes 10 million – a ten-fold increase since 1648.[1]

Statistics in the rest of the Americas are not so striking. Both immigration and innovation were less than impetuous and, though the population tripled, one quarter of this gain was merely a recovery to the pre-Columban level and another quarter due to the import of Negro slaves.

There was one other area of the world where new land was freely available, the Indonesian archipelago. Population increase there was at least 100 per cent. In most of the rest of the world there was not enough free land to support growth at this rate; more intensive or efficient working of the old was also necessary. In China for example the population rose 100 per cent but the area of cultivated land by only 50 per cent; there may have been some improvement in agricultural techniques, but the bulk of the increase in yield necessary to support the higher density of population came from a more intensive use of labour. The pattern of agricultural changes underlying Europe's population increase (also 100 per cent) is discussed overleaf.

In the remainder of the world population growth was held down by shortage of land (the Japanese managed only a 50 per cent rise) and stagnant technology (India, also in the 50 per cent bracket and the Near East as usual at the bottom of the league with 33 per cent). For Africa I have postulated a 33 per cent increase. This figure – which is no more than a guess – implies an absolute increase of around 14 million. The number removed from the area by the slave traders was almost as large: a reasonable estimate is 10 million. Surprisingly the modern view is that this probably made little difference to Africa's population growth, which was limited by other factors than fertility.[2]

Note that in absolute terms the bulk of the increase was still coming in the areas with the densest populations. China, Japan, India and Europe were between them responsible for more than 80 per cent of the rise since 1648 and still contained 80 per cent of the world's population in 1815.[3]

2. Between 1648 and 1815 about one million Negroes were shipped from the east coast of Africa to the Arab world and 9 million from the west coast to the Americas. The slave population of the Americas at the end of the period was around 5 million, of whom 1·5 million were in the southern United States, 1 million in the Caribbean and 2 million in Brazil. Excluded from the total are the third of a million ex-slaves who formed the population of Haiti.

The slave trade was formally abolished by the British and Americans in 1807–8. Other nations dragged their heels and the abolition became effective only in the 1840s, when the main importing country, Brazil, agreed to put an end to the traffic.

3. The first step in the colonization of Australia was made shortly before the end of our period when the British, having lost their American dumping ground, decided to establish a penal settlement at Botany Bay (near Sydney, New South Wales). That was in 1788. The first free settlers arrived in 1793 and the population built up to 30,000 by 1820.

Australia had been accidentally discovered by the Dutch in the early seventeenth century. They found the best way to Indonesia was to sail due east from the Cape of Good Hope and only turn north at the last moment. This enabled them to spend most of the voyage in the 'roaring forties', the latitudes where the winds are strong and westerly, and so cut the journey time (Amsterdam to Batavia) from eighteen months to six (see track on Map 49). The northward turn required the estimation of the ship's longitude which, prior to the introduction of the marine chronometer at the end of the eighteenth century, was a very approximate business. Because of this, Dutch ships often overshot and came to grief on the desolate west coast of Australia.

Some deliberate exploration followed the discovery, but when the north and south coasts proved equally barren the interest of V.O.C.'s cost-conscious directors evaporated. Their last major effort was Tasman's expedition of 1642. Tasman took a low 'roaring forties' course and passed south of most of Australia. At this point he hit on Tasmania, then, 1,200 miles further east, New Zealand (both off this map; see map 17). He then turned north to reach Batavia via the north coast of New Guinea. The voyage put a limit to the eastward extent of Australia and effectively completed the outline map of the world. There were still big gaps but, with the exception of Antarctica, they all turned out to be empty.

1. The Americans were very proud of their explosive demography. At the time of the revolution a patriot calculated that the colonies' population would pass the mother country's within twenty years and double it within fifty. Historians are an innumerate lot but they do know that America's population has been bigger than Britain's for some time, so the prediction is always quoted with approval. In fact, apart from getting the trend right (and who could have got it wrong?), the prediction was lousy. Fifty years later it was the United Kingdom that had twice the population of the United States, and England alone still contained more people (12 million) than America and Canada combined (11 million).

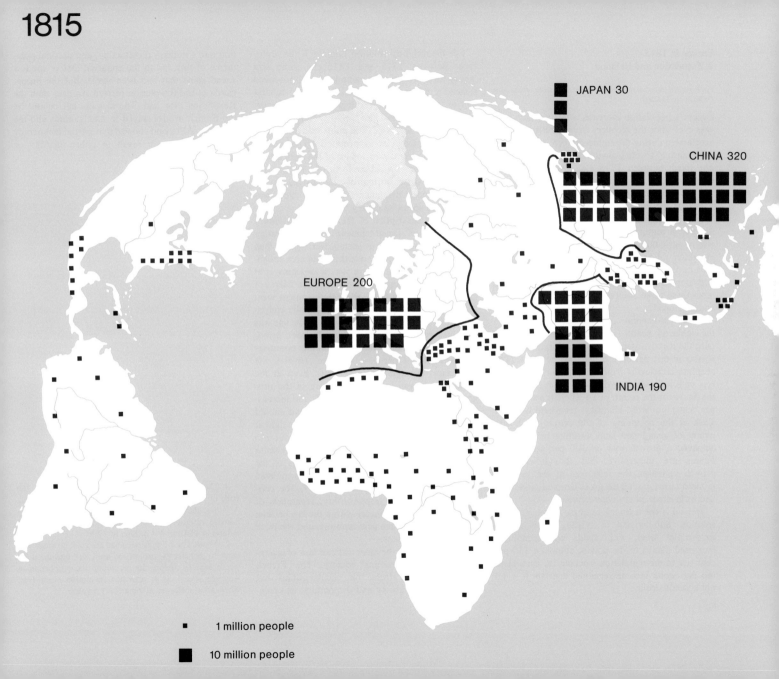

1815

JAPAN 30

CHINA 320

EUROPE 200

INDIA 190

■ 1 million people

■ 10 million people

Each symbol represents 1 million people, Catholic, Protestant, Orthodox or Moslem

Europe's population increase, a fairly steady process ever since the recovery from the Black Death, accelerated during the eighteenth century. Between 1600 and 1715 the growth had been just short of one third: between 1715 and 1815 it was over three quarters. At the end of the period the total was just over the 200 million mark.

Before the era of food imports from the New World (which began to be important only in the nineteenth century) a rise in population required a rise in agricultural output. There were three ways in which this could be achieved: increasing the area under cultivation, increasing the labour force and improving agricultural technology. Let us label these three solutions 'extensive', 'intensive' and 'technical'.

A perfect example of the extensive solution in the eighteenth century is the movement of peasants onto the Russian steppe. The growth rate for South Russia in this period touched 400 per cent. (The absolute increase is from 5 to 20 million: as the rest of Russia was growing at a much slower rate the figure for the country as a whole is around 100 per cent.) Similarly, Hungary, recovered from the Turk at the beginning of the century and with plenty of abandoned land awaiting new settlers, achieved a growth rate of 300 per cent. These figures are impressive, but though extensive growth increased the resources of the state (in modern terms, put up the gross national product) it had little effect on *per capita* income.

Ireland is the textbook example of the intensive solution. Sub-division of existing farms to the garden-plot level, with yields correspondingly increased thanks to the potato, allowed a 150 per cent rise in the population working the land. Here too *per capita* income remained constant if it did not actually decline.[1]

For the technical solution England is the prototype. Between 1715 and 1815 the same size labour force working the same land area produced a steadily increasing amount of food. In the first half of the century the result was a sizable export surplus, in the second half the rise in total population absorbed the extra. The point was that a 100 per cent increase in labour productivity had greatly increased the *per capita* wealth of the agricultural sector. This was the achievement of a society that consciously strove to improve its farming by upgrading stock, machinery and land and was prepared to spend its money to do so.

The cant description of the eighteenth century as the 'Age of Enlightenment' implies a rather more complete victory of reason over bigotry than was in fact the case. For one thing the area enlightened was restricted. There was a widening split between the northern and Mediterranean halves of Europe and in the latter the enlightenment went almost entirely unperceived. The Catholic church lost little of its authority and its overall decline was largely a reflection of the relatively poor demographic performance of the Catholic countries (averaging a 50 per cent increase) *vis-à-vis* the Protestant (averaging 75 per cent). Even in the north, which was increasingly aware of the progress of human knowledge and skills and increasingly aware that this progress could and should be encouraged, it was a matter of seeing the light at the end of the tunnel rather than bursting out into the sun. The only society to break out in any sense was in the New World. There the ideas of the intellectual *avant garde* of Europe were formulated in the American constitution of 1787. The concepts of democratic responsibility, separation of church and state and liberty within the law became the foundations of the new republic, and the birth right of all its citizens.

Old Europe had the more difficult task of changing an already existing society. The French Revolution was strong on secularization but always weak on liberty and democracy: its evolution into a military dictatorship, and the final overthrow of this, led to the apparent loss of the few social gains that had been made. But the propaganda of the Revolution proved stronger than the Revolution ever had. The slogans left behind by the French armies stayed in men's minds and the example of England showed that partial democracy did not necessarily result in either anarchy or tyranny.[2]

1. The dangers of monoculture caught up with the Irish in 1845 when potato blight arrived from America. A famine that cost over a million lives was followed by massive emigration: the population declined from 8·5 million in 1848 to 4·4 million in 1900.

2. About 1 in 8 Englishmen had the vote: no move was made to increase the proportion until well into the nineteenth century. Before the revolution the proportion in America was 1 in 4: after the revolution every free, white, adult male was automatically a voter.

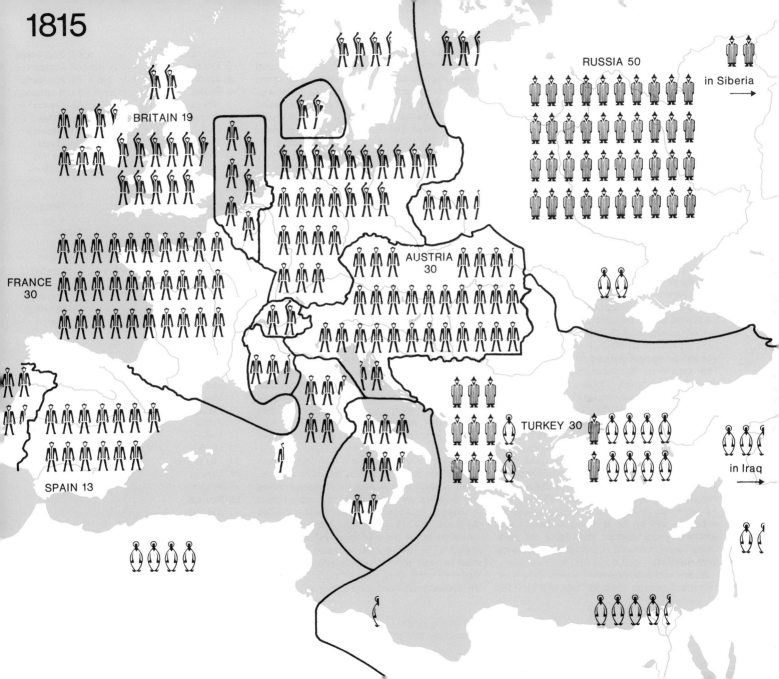

1815

BRITAIN 19

RUSSIA 50

in Siberia

FRANCE
30

AUSTRIA
30

SPAIN 13

TURKEY 30

in Iraq

Europe in 1815
3. Towns, Trade and Revenues

Towns grew fast in the eighteenth century. By 1815 there were so many in the lowest of the five ranks shown on the map that there is no room for their names and I have had to number them. At the other end of the scale London passed the million mark, the first city in the world to do so. In percentage terms the process of urbanization is somewhat less impressive because of the rise in total population. The figure for Western Europe as a whole is 10 per cent, which means that Italy has become an averagely rather than an exceptionally urbanized country. The Low Countries are still ahead of the game, but at 15 per cent show no advance on their proportion a century earlier. France and Spain are the laggards with 5 to 6 per cent, England and Scotland the leaders with 20 per cent.

The rapid urbanization of England and Scotland is a reflection of their industrial growth. It was in the second half of the eighteenth century that this process moved from the margin of the island's economy towards its centre; in the first half Britain was still an agricultural and commercial society. This is not to say that demand was stagnant in the earlier period: between 1715 and 1760 annual iron consumption (mostly for agricultural use) rose from 30,000 tons to 60,000; annual coal production (mostly for the domestic hearth) from 3 million to 6 million tons. By 1760 Britain had displaced the Dutch Republic as the country with the highest *per capita* income in Europe. At this stage Britain was not exporting any significant amount of manufactures. Imports (of Swedish and Russian iron and of the Baltic timber needed for shipbuilding) were paid for by the sale of English woollens and grain, and by the re-export of Eastern and American goods (cottons from India, tea from China, sugar from the Caribbean and tobacco from America).

In this confident, expanding society there were men with capital to invest and men with ideas for

investment. Understandably it was a collier who provided the £250,000 necessary to build a canal connecting his coal mines with the growing towns of Manchester and Liverpool (halving the cost of coal at the delivery point and vastly increasing sales). But it was the city of London and the squire-archy at large that financed the wave of canal building that followed. Probably half the 1,000 miles of canal built in the last half of the century never really repaid its cost. What the mania showed was the entrepreneurial resources available.

An obvious place for investment to pay off was in the iron industry. With home production crippled by the shortage of charcoal Britain was importing more than half the iron she used. Abraham Darby had shown that coke smelting of iron ore was possible, but a series of complementary innovations were needed to make a coal-based industry economic: the end product had to be competitive with Swedish iron in quality and Russian iron in price. The final links in the chain were completed in the 1780s. As a result iron production rose from 30,000 tons in 1760 to 125,000 tons in 1800 while, from an amount equivalent to total home production, net imports fell to zero. But the really startling gain came in the opening decade of the next century. By 1815 British iron-working capacity had risen to a million tons a year – more than the rest of Europe put together. By then British coal production was 15 million tons annually – more than five times that of the rest of Europe.

The expansion of Britain's traditional export industry, the textile trade, was just as remarkable. Wool production was near its economic ceiling and there was no possibility of increasing output by dramatic multiples: cotton was the fibre that fed the boom. In 1775 cotton represented only 5 per cent of the British textile business and exports were negligible. In 1800 exports of cotton goods were equal in value to exports of woollens. By 1815 they were worth three times as much. Technically the breakthrough was in spinning: until cotton-

1	Aberdeen	44	Nuremberg
2	Dundee	45	Stuttgart
3	Paisley	46	Augsburg
4	Belfast	47	Bergamo
5	Newcastle	48	Brescia
6	Oldham	49	Padua
7	Hull	50	Piacenza
8	Stoke	51	Parma
9	Wolverhampton	52	Ferrara
10	Nottingham	53	Leghorn
11	Norwich	54	Constantine
12	Bath	55	Riga
13	Portsmouth	56	Danzig
14	Amiens	57	Vilna
15	Caen	58	Orel
16	Reims	59	Tula
17	Metz	60	Kazan
18	Nancy	61	Saratov
19	Orleans	62	Kiev
20	Angers	63	Pressburg
21	Nîmes	64	Debrecen
22	Montpellier	65	Szeged
23	Toulon	66	Belgrade
24	Valladolid	67	Bucarest
25	Ecija	68	Adrianople
26	Cordova	69	Salonika
27	Jaén	70	Konya
28	Murcia	71	Kayseri
29	Cartagena		
30	Palma		
31	Meknes		
32	Leyden		
33	The Hague		
34	Utrecht		
35	Bruges		
36	Tournai		
37	Aachen		
38	Cologne		
39	Bremen		
40	Brunswick		
41	Magdeburg		
42	Leipzig		
43	Frankfurt		

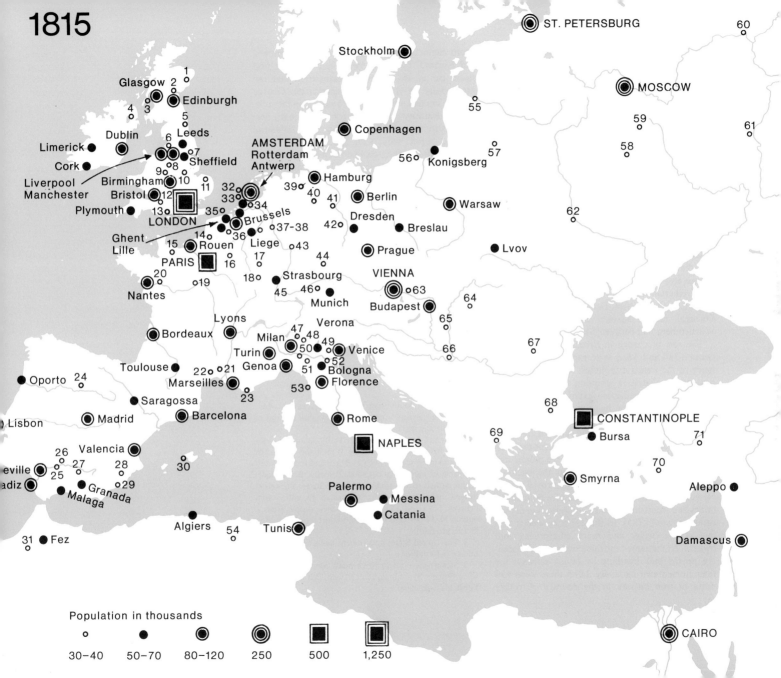

1815

ST. PETERSBURG
60
Stockholm
MOSCOW
55
59
61
58
Glasgow 1
2
Edinburgh
4
3
Copenhagen
5
Leeds
56 Konigsberg
57
Dublin 6
Limerick
7
Sheffield
Hamburg
Warsaw
Cork
8
AMSTERDAM
62
9
Rotterdam
Liverpool
Antwerp
39
40
Berlin
Manchester
Birmingham 10
11
41
Bristol 12
32
Lvov
Plymouth 13
33
34
Dresden
Breslau
LONDON
35
Brussels
42
Ghent
36
37-38
Prague
Lille
14
Liege
43
VIENNA
15
Rouen
17
44
63
PARIS
16
45
46
Strasbourg
64
20
18
Budapest
19
Munich
65
Nantes
66
Lyons
Verona
67
Bordeaux
47
48
Milan
50
49
Turin
52
Venice
Toulouse
22
21
51
Bologna
68
CONSTANTINOPLE
Marseilles
Genoa
Florence
Oporto 24
23
53
69
Bursa
Saragossa
Rome
71
Lisbon
Madrid
Barcelona
NAPLES
70
26
Valencia
Smyrna
eville
27
28
30
Aleppo
25
29
adiz
Granada
Palermo
Messina
Malaga
Catania
31 Fez
Algiers 54
Tunis
Damascus
CAIRO

Population in thousands

○	●	◉	◎	◻	▣
30-40	50-70	80-120	250	500	1,250

wool could be spun cheaply its potential cost advantage over animal wool was hardly realizable in practice. With the introduction of Hargreaves eight-spindle machine in 1767 the productivity of the individual worker immediately increased eight times. By 1790 eighty-spindle machines were in use, the quality of machine-spun yarn had improved out of all recognition and its cost had fallen to a tenth of the hand-spun equivalent. The 'mill' which has become the symbol of the 'industrial revolution' was a factory housing water-driven spinning machines.[1]

The growth of British agriculture and industry and the degree to which they were outpacing their equivalents on the continent is demonstrated by the figures for government revenues in 1815. At £70m. Britain stands clear of the field: France has less than half as much – £32m. Far behind are Russia and Austria (£10m. each), Prussia (£7m.), the Netherlands (£6m.) and Spain and Naples (£3·5m. each). Bavaria, Denmark, the Papal State, Portugal, Savoy, Saxony, Sweden, Turkey and Württemberg had between £1m. and £2m. each.[2]

The rate of change in Britain in the years between 1780 and 1815 is so rapid and the importance of the trends established so obvious for the next period that it is tempting to overstress the degree of industrialization existing in 1815. But though by then Britain had a larger industrial and commercial sector than any other nation, 40 per cent of the population still worked on the land. Though much less than the 80 per cent that was the norm in Europe, this is still a large proportion. Even more seductive is the appeal of the machines themselves. Watt not only greatly improved the old Newcomen steam engine, long used for pumping in mines and ironworks, he also equipped it to deliver rotary power (1785). In this form he sold it to a few of the bigger and more enterprising mill owners. At the same time mine owners were speeding up the bulk handling by laying railways for their horsedrawn carts. By 1815 there were 150 miles of iron railway in the country. A rotary

steam engine and a railway are obvious partners, and Richard Trevithick, who had built the first steam car in 1801, built a steam train that ran successfully in 1804. Ten years later George Stephenson had a practical locomotive on the rails. But the Railway Age, which for the ordinary person was to mark the inauguration of the industrial society, began only with the opening of the Stockton and Darlington line in Durham ten years after the end of our period.[3] In 1815 England still had more green fields than satanic mills; the Royal Navy ruled the waves with wooden ships not very different from those of a hundred years earlier, and only the most far-sighted realized that coal, iron and steam were creating a new nation and a new world.

1. The power loom existed but only as a rarity: weaving remained largely a cottage industry until the end of the Napoleonic wars.
The British cotton industry originally obtained its raw material from plantations in the West Indies but when these (and other sources such as Brazil and India) proved incapable of increasing output sufficiently, British merchants turned to the southern United States. Plantation owners there switched from tobacco to cotton and between 1795 and 1815 increased their output from 1 million lb. (4 per cent of British imports) to 55 million lb. (55 per cent).

2. The United States government had a revenue of £4 million (S 15 million).

3. Steam was used to drive boats as early as 1801, when William Symmington ran a steam-driven tug on the Forth & Clyde canal.

Index

The grid numbers following the name of towns etc. refer to the maps at the back of the book

Penguin Books Ltd, Harmondsworth, Middlesex, England
Viking Penguin Inc., 40 West 23rd Street, New York, New York 10010, U.S.A.
Penguin Books Australia Ltd, Ringwood, Victoria, Australia
Penguin Books Canada Ltd, 2801 John Street, Markham, Ontario, Canada L3R 1B4
Penguin Books (N.Z.) Ltd, 182-190 Wairau Road, Auckland 10, New Zealand

First published in 1972
Reprinted 1975, 1977, 1979, 1980, 1983, 1984, 1986, 1987

Printed in Hong Kong

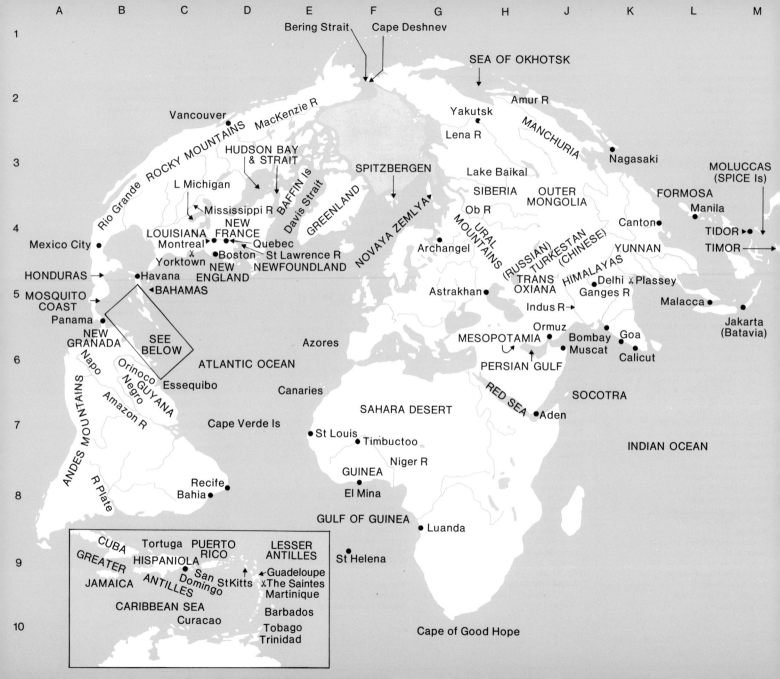